CONTENTS

Introduction

The Air Fryer Oven is an easy way to cook delicious healthy meals. Rather than cooking the food in oil and hot fat that may affect your health, the machine uses rapid hot air to circulate around and cook meals. This allows the outside of your food to be crispy and also makes sure that the inside layers are cooked through.

Air Fryer Oven allows us to cook almost everything and a lot of dishes. We can use the Air Fryer Oven to cook Meat, vegetables, poultry, fruit, fish and a wide variety of desserts. It is possible to prepare your entire meals, starting from appetizers to main courses as well as desserts. Not to mention, Air Fryer Oven also allows homemade preserves or even delicious sweets and cakes.

How Does Air Fryer Oven Works?

The technology of the Air Fryer Oven is very simple. Fried foods get their crunchy texture because hot oil heats foods quickly and evenly on their surface. Oil is an excellent heat conductor, which helps with fast and simultaneous cooking across all of the ingredients. For decades cooks have used convection ovens to try to mimic the effects of frying or cooking the whole surface of the food. But the air never circulates quickly enough to achieve that delicious surface crisp we all love in fried foods.

With this mechanism, the air is circulated on high degrees, up to 200° C, to "air fry" any food such as fish, chicken or chips, etc. This technology has changed the whole idea of cooking by reducing the fat up to 80% compared to old-fashioned deep fat frying.

The Air Fryer Oven cooking releases the heat through a heating element which cooks the food in a healthier and more appropriate way. There's also an exhaust fan right above the cooking chamber which provides the food required airflow. This way food is cooked with constant heated air. This leads to the same heating temperature reaching every single part of the food that is being cooked. So, this is only grill and the exhaust fan that is helping the Air Fryer Oven to boost air at a constantly high speed in order to cook healthy food with less fat.

The internal pressure increases the temperature that will then be controlled by the exhaust system. Exhaust fan also releases filtered extra air to cook the food in a much healthier way. Air Fryer Oven has no odor at all and it is absolutely harmless making it user and environment-friendly.

Benefits of the Air Fryer Oven

- Healthier, oil-free meals
- It eliminates cooking odors through internal air filters
- Makes cleaning easier due to lack of oil grease
- Air Fryer Ovens are able to bake, grill, roast and fry providing more options
- A safer method of cooking compared to deep frying with exposed hot oil
- Has the ability to set and leave as most models and it includes a digital timer

The Air Fryer Oven is an all-in-one that allows cooking to be easy and quick. It also leads to a lot of possibilities once you get to know it. Once you learn the basics and become familiar with your Air Fryer Oven, you can feel free to experiment and modify the recipes in the way you prefer. You can prepare a wide number of dishes in the Air Fryer Oven and you can adapt your favorite stove-top dish so it becomes Air Fryer Oven–friendly. It all boils down to variety and lots of options, right?

Cooking perfect and delicious as well as healthy meals has never been easier. You can see how this recipe collection proves itself.

Enjoy!

Vegetables Recipes

Air Fryer Asparagus

Prep: 5 Minutes • Cook Time: 8 Minutes • Total: 13 Minutes
Serves: 2
Ingredients
Nutritional yeast
Olive oil non-stick spray
One bunch of asparagus
Directions
1.   Wash asparagus and then trim off thick, woody ends.
2.   Spray asparagus with olive oil spray and sprinkle with yeast.
3.   Add the asparagus to air fryer rack/basket in a singular layer. Set temperature to 360°F, and set time to 8 minutes. Select START/STOP to begin.
PER SERVING: CALORIES: 17; FAT: 4G; PROTEIN: 9G

Almond Flour Battered And Crisped Onion Rings

Prep: 5 Minutes • Cook Time: 15 Minutes • Total: 20 Minutes
Serves: 3
Ingredients
½ cup almond flour
¾ cup coconut milk
1 big white onion, sliced into rings
1 egg, beaten
1 tablespoon baking powder
1 tablespoon smoked paprika
Salt and pepper to taste
Directions
1. Preheat the air fryer Oven for 5 minutes.
2. In a mixing bowl, mix the almond flour, baking powder, smoked paprika, salt and pepper.
3. In another bowl, combine the eggs and coconut milk.
4. Soak the onion slices into the egg mixture.
5. Dredge the onion slices in the almond flour mixture.
6. Pour into the Oven rack/basket. Set temperature to 325°F, and set time to 15 minutes. Select START/STOP to begin. Shake the fryer basket for even cooking.
PER SERVING: CALORIES: 217; FAT: 17.9G; PROTEIN: 5.3G

Jalapeño Poppers

Prep: 10 Minutes • Cook Time: 10 Minutes • Total: 20 Minutes
Serves: 4
Ingredients
12 whole fresh jalapeño
1 cup refried beans
1 cup extra-sharp cheddar cheese
1 scallion, sliced
1 teaspoon salt
1/4 cup all-purpose flour
2 large eggs
1/2 cup fine cornmeal
Olive oil or canola oil cooking spray

Directions
1.   Start by slicing each jalapeño lengthwise on one side. Place the jalapeños side by side in a microwave safe bowl and microwave them until they are slightly soft; usually around 5 minutes.
2.   While your jalapeños cook; mix refried beans, scallions, 1/2 teaspoon salt, and cheese in a bowl.
3.   Once your jalapeños are softened you can scoop out the seeds and add one tablespoon of your refried bean mixture (It can be a little less if the pepper is smaller.) Press the jalapeño closed around the filling.
4.   Beat your eggs in a small bowl and place your flour in a separate bowl. In a third bowl mix your cornmeal and the remaining salt in a third bowl.
5.   Roll each pepper in the flour, then dip it in the egg, and finally roll it in the cornmeal making sure to coat the entire pepper.
6.   Place the peppers on a flat surface and coat them with a cooking spray; olive oil cooking spray is suggested.
7.   Pour into the Oven rack/basket. Place the Rack on the middle-shelf of the Air fryer oven. Set temperature to 400°F, and set time to 5 minutes. Select START/STOP to begin. Turn each pepper, and then cook for another 5 minutes; serve hot.
PER SERVING: CALORIES: 244; FAT: 12G; PROTEIN: 12G; FIBER: 2.4G

Parmesan Breaded Zucchini Chips

Prep: 15 Minutes • Cook Time: 20 Minutes • Total: 35 Minutes
Serves: 5
Ingredients
For the zucchini chips:
2 medium zucchini
2 eggs
⅓ cup bread crumbs
⅓ cup grated Parmesan cheese
Salt
Pepper
Cooking oil
For the lemon aioli:
½ cup mayonnaise
½ tablespoon olive oil
Juice of ½ lemon
1 teaspoon minced garlic
Salt
Pepper
Directions
To make the zucchini chips:
1. Slice the zucchini into thin chips (about ⅛ inch thick) using a knife or mandoline.
2. In a small bowl, beat the eggs. In another small bowl, combine the bread crumbs, Parmesan cheese, and salt and pepper to taste.
3. Spray the air fryer basket with cooking oil.
4. Dip the zucchini slices one at a time in the eggs and then the bread crumb mixture. You can also sprinkle the bread crumbs onto the zucchini slices with a spoon.
5. Place the zucchini chips in the air fryer basket, but do not stack.
6. Pour into the Oven rack/basket. Place the Rack on the middle-shelf of the Air fryer oven. Cook in batches. Spray the chips with cooking oil from a distance (otherwise, the breading may fly off). Set temperature to 360°F and cook for 10 minutes.
7. Remove the cooked zucchini chips from the air fryer oven, then repeat with the remaining zucchini.
To make the lemon aioli:
1.   While the zucchini is cooking, combine the mayonnaise, olive oil, lemon juice, and garlic in a small bowl, adding salt and pepper to taste. Mix well until fully combined.
2.   Cool the zucchini and serve alongside the aioli.
PER SERVING: CALORIES: 192; FAT: 13G; PROTEIN: 6G; FIBER: 4G

Bell Pepper-Corn Wrapped in Tortilla

Prep: 5 Minutes • Cook Time: 15 Minutes • Total: 20 Minutes
Serves: 4
Ingredients
1 small red bell pepper, chopped
1 small yellow onion, diced
1 tablespoon water
2 cobs grilled corn kernels
4 large tortillas
4 pieces commercial vegan nuggets, chopped
mixed greens for garnish
Directions
1.   Preheat the air fryer oven to 400°F.
2.   In a skillet heated over medium heat, water sauté the vegan nuggets together with the onions, bell peppers, and corn kernels. Set aside.
3.   Place filling inside the corn tortillas.
4.   Pour the tortillas into the Oven rack/basket. Place the Rack on the middle-shelf of the Air fryer oven. Set temperature to 400°F, and set time to 15 minutes until the tortilla wraps are crispy.
5.   Serve with mix greens on top.
PER SERVING: CALORIES: 548; FAT: 20.7G; PROTEIN: 46G

Baked Cheesy Eggplant with Marinara

Prep: 5 Minutes • Cook Time: 45 Minutes • Total: 50 Minutes
Serves: 3
Ingredients
1 clove garlic, sliced
1 large eggplants
1 tablespoon olive oil
1 tablespoon olive oil
1/2 pinch salt, or as needed
1/4 cup and 2 tablespoons dry bread crumbs
1/4 cup and 2 tablespoons ricotta cheese
1/4 cup grated Parmesan cheese
1/4 cup grated Parmesan cheese
1/4 cup water, plus more as needed
1/4 teaspoon red pepper flakes
1-1/2 cups prepared marinara sauce
1-1/2 teaspoons olive oil
2 tablespoons shredded pepper jack cheese
salt and freshly ground black pepper to taste

Directions
1.   Cut eggplant crosswise in 5 pieces. Peel and chop two pieces into ½-inch cubes.
2.   Lightly grease baking pan of air fryer with 1 tbsp olive oil for 5 minutes, heat oil at 390°F. Add half eggplant strips and cook for 2 minutes per side. Transfer to a plate.
3.   Add 1 ½ tsp olive oil and add garlic. Cook for a minute. Add chopped eggplants. Season with pepper flakes and salt. Cook for 4 minutes. Lower heat to 330°F. and continue cooking eggplants until soft, around 8 minutes more.
4.   Stir in water and marinara sauce. Cook for 7 minutes until heated through. Stirring every now and then. Transfer to a bowl.
5.   In a bowl, whisk well pepper, salt, pepper jack cheese, Parmesan cheese, and ricotta. Evenly spread cheeses over eggplant strips and then fold in half.
6.   Lay folded eggplant in baking pan. Pour marinara sauce on top.
7.   In a small bowl whisk well olive oil, and bread crumbs. Sprinkle all over sauce.
8.   Place the baking dish in the Air fryer oven cooking basket. Cook for 15 minutes at 390°F until tops are lightly browned.
9.   Serve and enjoy.
PER SERVING: CALORIES: 405; FAT: 21.4G; PROTEIN: 12.7G

Spicy Sweet Potato Fries

Prep: 5 Minutes • Cook Time: 37 Minutes • Total: 45 Minutes
Serves: 4
Ingredients
2 tbsp. sweet potato fry seasoning mix
2 tbsp. olive oil
2 sweet potatoes
Seasoning Mix:
2 tbsp. salt
1 tbsp. cayenne pepper
1 tbsp. dried oregano
1 tbsp. fennel
2 tbsp. coriander
Directions:
1.   Slice both ends off sweet potatoes and peel. Slice lengthwise in half and again crosswise to make four pieces from each potato.
2.   Slice each potato piece into 2-3 slices, then slice into fries.
3.   Grind together all of seasoning mix ingredients and mix in the salt.
4.   Ensure the air fryer oven is preheated to 350 degrees.
5.   Toss potato pieces in olive oil, sprinkling with seasoning mix and tossing well to coat thoroughly.
6.   Add fries to air fryer basket. Set temperature to 350°F, and set time to 27 minutes. Select START/STOP to begin.
7.   Take out the basket and turn fries. Turn off air fryer and let cook 10-12 minutes till fries are golden.
PER SERVING: CALORIES: 89; FAT: 14G; PROTEIN: 8Gs; SUGAR:3G

Creamy Spinach Quiche

Prep: 10 Minutes • Cook Time: 20 Minutes • Total: 30 Minutes
Serves: 4
Ingredients
Premade quiche crust, chilled and rolled flat to a 7-inch round
eggs
¼ cup of milk
Pinch of salt and pepper
1 clove of garlic, peeled and finely minced
½ cup of cooked spinach, drained and coarsely chopped
¼ cup of shredded mozzarella cheese
¼ cup of shredded cheddar cheese
Directions
1.   Preheat the air fryer oven to 360 degrees.
2.   Press the premade crust into a 7-inch pie tin, or any appropriately sized glass or ceramic heat-safe dish. Press and trim at the edges if necessary. With a fork, pierce several holes in the dough to allow air circulation and prevent cracking of the crust while cooking.
3.   In a mixing bowl, beat the eggs until fluffy and until the yolks and white are evenly combined.
4.   Add milk, garlic, spinach, salt and pepper, and half the cheddar and mozzarella cheese to the eggs. Set the rest of the cheese aside for now, and stir the mixture until completely blended. Make sure the spinach is not clumped together, but rather spread among the other ingredients.
5.   Pour the mixture into the pie crust, slowly and carefully to avoid splashing. The mixture should almost fill the crust, but not completely – leaving a ¼ inch of crust at the edges.
6.   Place the baking dish in the Air fryer oven cooking basket. Set the air fryer oven timer for 15 minutes. After15 minutes, the air fryer will shut off, and the quiche will already be firm and the crust beginning to brown. Sprinkle the rest of the cheddar and mozzarella cheese on top of the quiche filling. Reset the air fryer oven at 360 degrees for 5 minutes. After 5 minutes, when the air fryer shuts off, the cheese will have formed an exquisite crust on top and the quiche will be golden brown and perfect. Remove from the air fryer using oven mitts or tongs, and set on a heat-safe surface to cool for a few minutes before cutting.

Air Fryer Cauliflower Rice

Prep: 5 Minutes • Cook Time: 20 Minutes • Total: 25 Minutes
Serves: 4
Ingredients
Round 1:
tsp. turmeric
1 C. diced carrot
½ C. diced onion
2 tbsp. low-sodium soy sauce
½ block of extra firm tofu
Round 2:
½ C. frozen peas
2 minced garlic cloves
½ C. chopped broccoli
1 tbsp. minced ginger
1 tbsp. rice vinegar
1 ½ tsp. toasted sesame oil
2 tbsp. reduced-sodium soy sauce
3 C. riced cauliflower
Directions:
1. Crumble tofu in a large bowl and toss with all the Round one ingredient.
2. Preheat the air fryer oven to 370 degrees, place the baking dish in the Air fryer oven cooking basket, set temperature to 370°F, and set time to 10 minutes and cook 10 minutes, making sure to shake once.
3. In another bowl, toss ingredients from Round 2 together.
4. Add Round 2 mixture to air fryer and cook another 10 minutes, ensuring to shake 5 minutes in.
5. Enjoy!
PER SERVING: CALORIES: 67; FAT: 8G; PROTEIN: 3G

Brown Rice, Spinach and Tofu Frittata

Prep: 5 Minutes • Cook Time: 55 Minutes • Total: 60 Minutes
Serves: 4
Ingredients
½ cup baby spinach, chopped
½ cup kale, chopped
½ onion, chopped
½ teaspoon turmeric
1 ¾ cups brown rice, cooked
1 flax egg (1 tablespoon flaxseed meal + 3 tablespoon cold water)
1 package firm tofu
1 tablespoon olive oil
1 yellow pepper, chopped
2 tablespoons soy sauce
2 teaspoons arrowroot powder
2 teaspoons Dijon mustard
2/3 cup almond milk
3 big mushrooms, chopped
3 tablespoons nutritional yeast
4 cloves garlic, crushed
4 spring onions, chopped
a handful of basil leaves, chopped
Directions:
1.   Preheat the air fryer oven to 375°F. Grease a pan that will fit inside the air fryer oven.
2.   Prepare the frittata crust by mixing the brown rice and flax egg. Press the rice onto the baking dish until you form a crust. Brush with a little oil and cook for 10 minutes.
3.   Meanwhile, heat olive oil in a skillet over medium flame and sauté the garlic and onions for 2 minutes.
4.   Add the pepper and mushroom and continue stirring for 3 minutes.
5.   Stir in the kale, spinach, spring onions, and basil. Remove from the pan and set aside.
6.   In a food processor, pulse together the tofu, mustard, turmeric, soy sauce, nutritional yeast, vegan milk and arrowroot powder. Pour in a mixing bowl and stir in the sautéed vegetables.
7.   Pour the vegan frittata mixture over the rice crust and cook in the air fryer oven for 40 minutes.
PER SERVING: CALORIES: 226; FAT: 8.05G; PROTEIN: 10.6G

Stuffed Mushrooms

Prep: 7 Minutes • Cook Time: 8 Minutes • Total: 15 Minutes
Serves: 12
Ingredients
2 Rashers Bacon, Diced
½ Onion, Diced
½ Bell Pepper, Diced
1 Small Carrot, Diced
24 Medium Size Mushrooms (Separate the caps & stalks)
1 cup Shredded Cheddar Plus Extra for the Top
½ cup Sour Cream
Directions:
1. Chop the mushrooms stalks finely into the Oven rack/basket. Place the Rack on the middle-shelf of the Air fryer oven. Set temperature to 350°F, and set time to 8 minutes and fry them up with the bacon, onion, pepper and carrot. When the veggies are fairly tender, stir in the sour cream & the cheese. Keep on the heat until the cheese has melted and everything is mixed nicely.
2. Now grab the mushroom caps and heap a plop of filling on each one.
3. Place in the fryer basket and top with a little extra cheese.

Air Fried Carrots, Yellow Squash & Zucchini

Prep: 5 Minutes • Cook Time: 35 Minutes • Total: 40 Minutes
Serves: 4

Ingredients

1 tbsp. chopped tarragon leaves
½ tsp. white pepper
1 tsp. salt
1 pound yellow squash
1 pound zucchini
6 tsp. olive oil
½ pound carrots

Directions:

1. Stem and root the end of squash and zucchini and cut in ¾-inch half-moons. Peel and cut carrots into 1-inch cubes
2. Combine carrot cubes with 2 teaspoons of olive oil, tossing to combine.
3. Pour into the air fryer oven basket, set temperature to 400°F, and set time to 5 minutes.
4. As carrots cook, drizzle remaining olive oil over squash and zucchini pieces, then season with pepper and salt. Toss well to coat.
5. Add squash and zucchini when the timer for carrots goes off. Cook 30 minutes, making sure to toss 2-3 times during the cooking process.
6. Once done, take out veggies and toss with tarragon. Serve up warm.

PER SERVING: CALORIES: 122; FAT: 9G; PROTEIN: 6G

Winter Vegetarian Frittata

Prep: 5 Minutes • Cook Time: 30 Minutes • Total: 35 Minutes
Serves: 4

Ingredients

1 leek, peeled and thinly sliced into rings
2 cloves garlic, finely minced
3 medium-sized carrots, finely chopped
2 tablespoons olive oil
6 large-sized eggs
Sea salt and ground black pepper, to taste
1/2 teaspoon dried marjoram, finely minced
1/2 cup yellow cheese of choice

Directions:

1. Sauté the leek, garlic, and carrot in hot olive oil until they are tender and fragrant; reserve.
2. In the meantime, preheat your air fryer oven to 330 degrees F.
3. In a bowl, whisk the eggs along with the salt, ground black pepper, and marjoram.
4. Then, grease the inside of your baking dish with a nonstick cooking spray. Pour the whisked eggs into the baking dish. Stir in the sautéed carrot mixture. Top with the cheese shreds.
5. Place the baking dish in the air fryer oven cooking basket. Cook about 30 minutes and serve warm.

Brussels Sprouts with Balsamic Oil

Prep: 5 Minutes • Cook Time: 15 Minutes • Total: 20 Minutes
Serves: 4
Ingredients
¼ teaspoon salt
1 tablespoon balsamic vinegar
2 cups Brussels sprouts, halved
tablespoons olive oil
Directions:
1.   Preheat the air fryer oven for 5 minutes.
2.   Mix all ingredients in a bowl until the zucchini fries are well coated.
3.   Place in the air fryer oven basket.
4.   Close and cook for 15 minutes for 350°F.
PER SERVING: CALORIES: 82; FAT: 6.8G; PROTEIN: 1.5G

Air Fried Kale Chips

Prep: 5 Minutes • Cook Time: 10 Minutes • Total: 15 Minutes
Serves: 6
Ingredients
¼ tsp. Himalayan salt
3 tbsp. yeast
Avocado oil
1 bunch of kale
Directions:
1.   Rinse kale and with paper towels, dry well.
2.   Tear kale leaves into large pieces. Remember they will shrink as they cook so good sized pieces are necessary.
3.   Place kale pieces in a bowl and spritz with avocado oil till shiny. Sprinkle with salt and yeast.
4.   With your hands, toss kale leaves well to combine.
5.   Pour half of the kale mixture into the air fryer oven basket, set temperature to 350°F, and set time to 5 minutes. Remove and repeat with another half of kale.
PER SERVING: CALORIES: 55; FAT: 10G; PROTEIN: 1G; SUGAR:0G

Zucchini Omelet

Prep: 10 Minutes • Cook Time: 10 Minutes • Total: 20 Minutes
Serves: 2
Ingredients
1 teaspoon butter
1 zucchini, julienned
4 eggs
¼ teaspoon fresh basil, chopped
¼ teaspoon red pepper flakes, crushed
Salt and freshly ground black pepper, to taste
Directions:
1.   Preheat the air fryer oven to 355 degrees F.
2.   In a skillet, melt butter on medium heat.
3.   Add zucchini and cook for about 3-4 minutes.
4.   In a bowl, add the eggs, basil, red pepper flakes, salt and black pepper and beat well.
5.   Add cooked zucchini and gently, stir to combine.
6.   Transfer the mixture into the air fryer oven pan.
7.   Cook for about 10 minutes or till done completely

Cheesy Cauliflower Fritters

Prep: 10 Minutes • Cook Time: 7 Minutes • Total: 17 Minutes
Serves: 8
Ingredients
½ C. chopped parsley
1 C. Italian breadcrumbs
1/3 C. shredded mozzarella cheese
1/3 C. shredded sharp cheddar cheese
1 egg
2 minced garlic cloves
3 chopped scallions
1 head of cauliflower
Directions:
1.   Cut cauliflower up into florets. Wash well and pat dry. Place into a food processor and pulse 20-30 seconds till it looks like rice.
2.   Place cauliflower rice in a bowl and mix with pepper, salt, egg, cheeses, breadcrumbs, garlic, and scallions.
3.   With hands, form 15 patties of the mixture. Add more breadcrumbs if needed.
4.   With olive oil, spritz patties, and place into your air fryer oven basket in a single layer. Set temperature to 390°F, and set time to 7 minutes, flipping after 7 minutes.
PER SERVING: CALORIES: 209; FAT: 17G; PROTEIN: 6G; SUGAR:0.5

Cauliflower Bites

Prep: 10 Minutes • Cook Time: 18 Minutes • Total: 28 Minutes
Serves: 4
Ingredients
1 Head Cauliflower, cut into small florets
Tsps Garlic Powder
Pinch of Salt and Pepper
1 Tbsp Butter, melted
1/2 Cup Chili Sauce
Olive Oil
Directions:
1.   Place cauliflower into a bowl and pour oil over florets to lightly cover.
2.   Season florets with salt, pepper and the garlic powder and toss well.
3.   Place florets into the air fryer oven at 350 degrees for 14 minutes.
4.   Remove cauliflower from the Air Fryer.
5.   Combine the melted butter with the chili sauce
6.   Pour over the florets so that they are well coated.
7.   Return to the air fryer oven and cook for additional 3 to 4 minutes
8.   Serve as a side or with ranch or cheese dip as a snack

Buttered Carrot-Zucchini with Mayo

Prep: 10 Minutes • Cook Time: 25 Minutes • Total: 35 Minutes
Serves: 4
Ingredients
1 tablespoon grated onion
2 tablespoons butter, melted
1/2-pound carrots, sliced
1-1/2 zucchinis, sliced
1/4 cup water
1/4 cup mayonnaise
1/4 teaspoon prepared horseradish
1/4 teaspoon salt
1/4 teaspoon ground black pepper
1/4 cup Italian bread crumbs
Directions:
1.   Lightly grease baking pan of air fryer with cooking spray. Add carrots. For 8 minutes, cook on 360°F. Add zucchini and continue cooking for another 5 minutes.
2.   Meanwhile, in a bowl whisk well pepper, salt, horseradish, onion, mayonnaise, and water. Pour into pan of veggies. Toss well to coat.
3.   In a small bowl mix melted butter and bread crumbs. Sprinkle over veggies.
4.   Pour into the Oven rack/basket. Place the Rack on the middle-shelf of the Air fryer oven. Set temperature to 490°F, and set time to 10 minutes until tops are lightly browned.
5.   Serve and enjoy.
PER SERVING: CALORIES: 223; FAT: 17G; PROTEIN: 2.7G; SUGAR:0.5

Avocado Fries

Prep: 10 Minutes • Cook Time: 7 Minutes • Total: 17 Minutes
Serves: 6
Ingredients
1 avocado
½ tsp. salt
½ C. panko breadcrumbs
Bean liquid (aquafaba) from a 15-ounce can of white or garbanzo beans
Directions:
1.   Peel, pit, and slice up avocado.
2.   Toss salt and breadcrumbs together in a bowl. Place aquafaba into another bowl.
3.   Dredge slices of avocado first in aquafaba and then in panko, making sure you get an even coating.
4.   Place coated avocado slices into a single layer in the air fryer oven b5asket. Set temperature to 390°F, and set time to 5 minutes.
5.   Serve with your favorite keto dipping sauce
PER SERVING: CALORIES: 102; FAT: 22G; PROTEIN:9G; SUGAR:1G

Roasted Vegetables Salad

Prep: 5 Minutes • Cook Time: 85 Minutes • Total: 90 Minutes
Serves: 5
Ingredients
3 eggplants
1 tbsp of olive oil
3 medium zucchini
1 tbsp of olive oil
4 large tomatoes, cut them in eighths
4 cups of one shaped pasta
2 peppers of any color
1 cup of sliced tomatoes cut into small cubes
2 teaspoon of salt substitute
8 tbsp of grated parmesan cheese
½ cup of Italian dressing
Leaves of fresh basil

Directions:
1. Wash your eggplant and slice it off then discard the green end. Make sure not to peel.
2. Slice your eggplant into1/2 inch of thick rounds. 1/2 inch)
3. Pour 1tbsp of olive oil on the eggplant round.
4. Put the eggplants in the basket of the air fryer and then toss it in the air fryer oven. Cook the eggplants for 40 minutes. Set the heat to 360 ° F
5. Meanwhile, wash your zucchini and slice it then discard the green end. But do not peel it.
6. Slice the Zucchini into thick rounds of ½ inch each.
7. In the basket of the Air Fryer, toss your ingredients
8. Add 1 tbsp of olive oil.
9. Cook the zucchini for 25 minutes on a heat of 360° F and when the time is off set it aside.
10. Wash and cut the tomatoes.
11. Arrange your tomatoes in the basket of the air fryer. Set the timer to 30 minutes. Set the heat to 350° F
12. When the time is off, cook your pasta according to the pasta guiding directions, empty it into a colander. Run the cold water on it and wash it and drain the pasta and put it aside.
13. Meanwhile, wash and chop your peppers and place it in a bow
14. Wash and thinly slice your cherry tomatoes and add it to the bowl. Add your roasted veggies.
15. Add the pasta, a pinch of salt, the topping dressing, add the basil and the parm and toss everything together. Set the ingredients together in the refrigerator, and let it chill
16. Serve your salad and enjoy it.

Cheddar, Squash And Zucchini Casserole

Prep: 5 Minutes • Cook Time: 30 Minutes • Total: 35 Minutes
Serves: 4
Ingredients
1 egg
5 saltine crackers, or as needed, crushed
2 tablespoons bread crumbs
1/2-pound yellow squash, sliced
1/2-pound zucchini, sliced
1/2 cup shredded Cheddar cheese
1-1/2 teaspoons white sugar
1/2 teaspoon salt
1/4 onion, diced
1/4 cup biscuit baking mix
1/4 cup butter

Directions:
1.   Lightly grease baking pan of air fryer with cooking spray. Add onion, zucchini, and yellow squash. Cover pan with foil and for 15 minutes, cook on 360° F or until tender.
2.   Stir in salt, sugar, egg, butter, baking mix, and cheddar cheese. Mix well. Fold in crushed crackers. Top with bread crumbs.
3.   Cook for 15 minutes at 390° F until tops are lightly browned.
4.   Serve and enjoy.

PER SERVING: CALORIES: 285; FAT: 20.5G; PROTEIN:8.6G

Zucchini Parmesan Chips

Prep: 10 Minutes • Cook Time: 8 Minutes • Total: 18 Minutes
Serves: 10
Ingredients
½ tsp. paprika
½ C. grated parmesan cheese
½ C. Italian breadcrumbs
1 lightly beaten egg
2 thinly sliced zucchinis

Directions:
1.   Use a very sharp knife or mandolin slicer to slice zucchini as thinly as you can. Pat off extra moisture.
2.   Beat egg with a pinch of pepper and salt and a bit of water.
3.   Combine paprika, cheese, and breadcrumbs in a bowl.
4.   Dip slices of zucchini into the egg mixture and then into breadcrumb mixture. Press gently to coat.
5.   With olive oil cooking spray, mist coated zucchini slices. Place into your air fryer oven basket in a single layer. Set temperature to 350°F, and set time to 8 minutes.
6.   Sprinkle with salt and serve with salsa.

PER SERVING: CALORIES: 211; FAT: 16G; PROTEIN:8G; SUGAR:0G

Jalapeño Cheese Balls

Prep: 10 Minutes • Cook Time: 8 Minutes • Total: 18 Minutes
Serves: 12
Ingredients
4 ounces cream cheese
⅓ cup shredded mozzarella cheese
⅓ cup shredded Cheddar cheese
2 jalapeños, finely chopped
½ cup bread crumbs
2 eggs
½ cup all-purpose flour
Salt
Pepper
Cooking oil
Directions:
1.   In a medium bowl, combine the cream cheese, mozzarella, Cheddar, and jalapeños. Mix well.
2.   Form the cheese mixture into balls about an inch thick. Using a small ice cream scoop works well.
3.   Arrange the cheese balls on a sheet pan and place in the freezer for 15 minutes. This will help the cheese balls maintain their shape while frying.
4.   Spray the air fryer oven basket with cooking oil. Place the bread crumbs in a small bowl. In another small bowl, beat the eggs. In a third small bowl, combine the flour with salt and pepper to taste, and mix well. Remove the cheese balls from the freezer. Dip the cheese balls in the flour, then the eggs, and then the bread crumbs.
5.   Place the cheese balls in the air fryer. Spray with cooking oil. Set temperature to 360°F. Cook for 8 minutes.
6.   Open the air fryer oven and flip the cheese balls. I recommend flipping them instead of shaking so the balls maintain their form. Cook an additional 4 minutes. Cool before serving.
PER SERVING: CALORIES: 96; FAT: 6G; PROTEIN:4G; SUGAR:0G

Crispy Roasted Broccoli

Prep: 10 Minutes • Cook Time: 8 Minutes • Total: 18 Minutes
Serves: 2
Ingredients
¼ tsp. Masala
½ tsp. red chili powder
½ tsp. salt
¼ tsp. turmeric powder
1 tbsp. chickpea flour
2 tbsp. yogurt
1 pound broccoli
Directions:
1.   Cut broccoli up into florets. Soak in a bowl of water with 2 teaspoons of salt for at least half an hour to remove impurities.
2.   Take out broccoli florets from water and let drain. Wipe down thoroughly.
3.   Mix all other ingredients together to create a marinade.
4.   Toss broccoli florets in the marinade. Cover and chill 15-30 minutes.
5.   Preheat the air fryer oven to 390 degrees. Place marinated broccoli florets into the fryer basket, set temperature to 350°F, and set time to 10 minutes. Florets will be crispy when done.
 PER SERVING: CALORIES: 96; FAT: 1.3G; PROTEIN:7G; SUGAR:4.5G

Creamy And Cheese Broccoli Bake

Prep: 5 Minutes • Cook Time: 30 Minutes • Total: 35 Minutes
Serves: 2
Ingredients
1-pound fresh broccoli, coarsely chopped
2 tablespoons all-purpose flour
salt to taste
1 tablespoon dry bread crumbs, or to taste
1/2 large onion, coarsely chopped
1/2 (14 ounce) can evaporated milk, divided
1/2 cup cubed sharp Cheddar cheese
1-1/2 teaspoons butter, or to taste
1/4 cup water
Directions:
1.   Lightly grease baking pan of air fryer with cooking spray. Mix in half of the milk and flour in pan and for 5 minutes, cook on 360°F. Halfway through cooking time, mix well. Add broccoli and remaining milk. Mix well and cook for another 5 minutes.
2.   Stir in cheese and mix well until melted.
3.   In a small bowl mix well, butter and bread crumbs. Sprinkle on top of broccoli.
4.   Place the baking pan in the Air fryer oven. Cook for 20 minutes at 360°F until tops are lightly browned.
5.   Serve and enjoy.
PER SERVING: CALORIES: 444; FAT: 22.3G; PROTEIN:23G

Coconut Battered Cauliflower Bites

Prep: 5 Minutes • Cook Time: 20 Minutes • Total: 25 Minutes
Serves: 4
Ingredients
salt and pepper to taste
1 flax egg (1 tablespoon flaxseed meal + 3 tablespoon water)
1 small cauliflower, cut into florets
1 teaspoon mixed spice
½ teaspoon mustard powder
2 tablespoons maple syrup
1 clove of garlic, minced
2 tablespoons soy sauce
1/3 cup oats flour
1/3 cup plain flour
1/3 cup desiccated coconut
Directions:
1.   Preheat the air fryer oven to 400°F.
2.   In a mixing bowl, mix together oats, flour, and desiccated coconut. Season with salt and pepper to taste. Set aside.
3.   In another bowl, place the flax egg and add a pinch of salt to taste. Set aside. Season the cauliflower with mixed spice and mustard powder.
4.   Dredge the florets in the flax egg first then in the flour mixture.
5.   Place inside the air fryer oven and cook for 15 minutes.
6.   Meanwhile, place the maple syrup, garlic, and soy sauce in a sauce pan and heat over medium flame. Bring to a boil and adjust the heat to low until the sauce thickens. After 15 minutes, take out the florets from the air fryer and place them in the saucepan.
7.   Toss to coat the florets and place inside the air fryer and cook for another 5 minutes.
PER SERVING: CALORIES: 154; FAT: 2.3G; PROTEIN:4.69G

Crispy Jalapeno Coins

Prep: 10 Minutes • Cook Time: 5 Minutes • Total: 15 Minutes
Serves: 2
Ingredients
1 egg
2-3 tbsp. coconut flour
1 sliced and seeded jalapeno
Pinch of garlic powder
Pinch of onion powder
Pinch of Cajun seasoning (optional)
Pinch of pepper and salt
Directions:
1.   Ensure your air fryer oven is preheated to 400 degrees.
2.   Mix together all dry ingredients.
3.   Pat jalapeno slices dry. Dip coins into egg wash and then into dry mixture. Toss to thoroughly coat.
4.   Add coated jalapeno slices to air fryer basket in a singular layer. Spray with olive oil.
5.   Set temperature to 350°F, and set time to 5 minutes. Cook just till crispy.
PER SERVING: CALORIES: 128; FAT: 8G; PROTEIN:7G; SUGAR:0G

Buffalo Cauliflower

Prep: 5 Minutes • Cook Time: 15 Minutes • Total: 20 Minutes
Serves: 2
Ingredients
Cauliflower:
1 C. panko breadcrumbs
1 tsp. salt
4 C. cauliflower florets
Buffalo Coating:
¼ C. Vegan Buffalo sauce
¼ C. melted vegan butter
Directions:
1.   Melt butter in microwave and whisk in buffalo sauce.
2.   Dip each cauliflower floret into buffalo mixture, ensuring it gets coated well. Hold over a bowl till floret is done dripping.
3.   Mix breadcrumbs with salt.
4.   Dredge dipped florets into breadcrumbs and place into air fryer basket. Set temperature to 350°F, and set time to 15 minutes. When slightly browned, they are ready to eat!
5.   Serve with your favorite keto dipping sauce.
PER SERVING: CALORIES: 194; FAT: 17G; PROTEIN:10G; SUGAR:3

Crisped Baked Cheese Stuffed Chile Pepper

Prep: 10 Minutes • Cook Time: 30 Minutes • Total: 40 Minutes
Serves: 3
Ingredients
1 (7 ounce) can whole green Chile peppers, drained
1 egg, beaten
1 tablespoon all-purpose flour
1/2 (5 ounce) can evaporated milk
1/2 (8 ounce) can tomato sauce
1/4-pound Monterey Jack cheese, shredded
1/4-pound Longhorn or Cheddar cheese, shredded
1/4 cup milk
Directions:
1.	Lightly grease baking pan of air fryer with cooking spray. Evenly spread chilies and sprinkle cheddar and Jack cheese on top.
2.	In a bowl whisk well flour, milk, and eggs. Pour over chilies.
3.	For 20 minutes, cook on 360°F
4.	Add tomato sauce on top.
5.	Cook for 10 minutes at 390°F until tops are lightly browned.
6.	Serve and enjoy.
PER SERVING: CALORIES: 392; FAT: 27.6G; PROTEIN:23.9G

Jicama Fries

Prep: 10 Minutes • Cook Time: 5 Minutes • Total: 15 Minutes
Serves: 8
Ingredients
1 tbsp. dried thyme
¾ C. arrowroot flour
½ large Jicama
eggs
Directions:
1.	Sliced jicama into fries.
2.	Whisk eggs together and pour over fries. Toss to coat.
3.	Mix a pinch of salt, thyme, and arrowroot flour together. Toss egg-coated jicama into dry mixture, tossing to coat well.
4.	Spray the air fryer oven basket with olive oil and add fries. Set temperature to 350°F, and set time to 5 minutes. Toss halfway into the cooking process.
PER SERVING: CALORIES: 211; FAT: 19G; PROTEIN:9G; SUGAR:1

Air Fryer Brussels Sprouts

Prep: 10 Minutes • Cook Time: 10 Minutes • Total: 20 Minutes
Serves: 8
Ingredients
¼ tsp. salt
1 tbsp. balsamic vinegar
1 tbsp. olive oil
2 C. Brussels sprouts
Directions:
1.	Cut Brussels sprouts in half lengthwise. Toss with salt, vinegar, and olive oil till coated thoroughly.
2.	Add coated sprouts to the air fryer oven, set temperature to 400°F, and set time to 10 minutes. Shake after 5 minutes of cooking.
3.	Brussels sprouts are ready to devour when brown and crisp.
PER SERVING: CALORIES: 118; FAT: 9G; PROTEIN:11G; SUGAR:1

Spaghetti Squash Tots

Prep: 10 Minutes • Cook Time: 15 Minutes • Total: 25 Minutes
Serves: 8
Ingredients
¼ tsp. pepper
½ tsp. salt
1 thinly sliced scallion
1 spaghetti squash
Directions:
1.   Wash and cut the squash in half lengthwise. Scrape out the seeds.
2.   With a fork, remove spaghetti meat by strands and throw out skins.
3.   In a clean towel, toss in squash and wring out as much moisture as possible. Place in a bowl and with a knife slice through meat a few times to cut up smaller.
4.   Add pepper, salt, and scallions to squash and mix well.
5.   Create "tot" shapes with your hands and place in the air fryer oven basket. Spray with olive oil. Set temperature to 350°F, and set time to 15 minutes. Cook until golden and crispy.
PER SERVING: CALORIES: 231; FAT: 18G; PROTEIN:5G; SUGAR:0G

Crispy And Healthy Avocado Fingers

Prep: 10 Minutes • Cook Time: 10 Minutes • Total: 20 Minutes
Serves: 4
Ingredients
½ cup panko breadcrumbs
½ teaspoon salt
1 pitted Haas avocado, peeled and sliced
liquid from 1 can white beans or aquafaba
Directions:
1.   Preheat the air fryer oven at 350°F.
2.   In a shallow bowl, toss the breadcrumbs and salt until well combined.
3.   Dredge the avocado slices first with the aquafaba then in the breadcrumb mixture.
4.   Place the avocado slices in a single layer inside the air fryer basket.
5.   Cook for 10 minutes and shake halfway through the cooking time.
PER SERVING: CALORIES: 51; FAT: 7.5G; PROTEIN:1.39G

Onion Rings

Serves: 4
Ingredients
1 large spanish onion
1/2 cup buttermilk
2 eggs, lightly beaten
3/4 cups unbleached all-purpose flour
3/4 cups panko bread crumbs
1/2 teaspoon baking powder
1/2 teaspoon Cayenne pepper, to taste
Salt

Directions:
1.   Start by cutting your onion into 1/2 thick rings and separate. Smaller pieces can be discarded or saved for other recipes.
2.   Beat the eggs in a large bowl and mix in the buttermilk, then set it aside.
3.   In another bowl combine flour, pepper, bread crumbs, and baking powder.
4.   Use a large spoon to dip a whole ring in the buttermilk, then pull it through the flour mix on both sides to completely coat the ring.
5.   Pour into the Oven rack/basket. Place the Rack on the middle-shelf of the Air fryer oven. Set temperature to 360°F, and set time to 8 minutes. Cook about 8 rings for 8-10 minutes at shaking half way through.
PER SERVING: CALORIES: 225; FAT: 3.8G; PROTEIN:19G; FIBER:2.4G

Cinnamon Butternut Squash Fries

Prep: 5 Minutes • Cook Time: 10 Minutes • Total: 15 Minutes
Serves: 8
Ingredients
1 pinch of salt
1 tbsp. powdered unprocessed sugar
½ tsp. nutmeg
2 tsp. cinnamon
1 tbsp. coconut oil
10 ounces pre-cut butternut squash fries
Directions:
1.   In a plastic bag, pour in all ingredients. Coat fries with other components till coated and sugar is dissolved.
2.   Spread coated fries into a single layer in the air fryer basket. Set temperature to 390°F, and set time to 10 minutes. Cook until crispy.
PER SERVING: CALORIES: 175; FAT: 8G; PROTEIN:1G; SUGAR

Poultry Recipes

Korean Chicken Wings

Prep: 5 Minutes • Cook Time: 10 Minutes • Total: 15 Minutes
Serves: 8
Ingredients
Wings:
1 tsp. pepper
1 tsp. salt
2 pounds chicken wings
Sauce:
2 packets Splenda
1 tbsp. minced garlic
1 tbsp. minced ginger
1 tbsp. sesame oil
1 tsp. agave nectar
1 tbsp. mayo
2 tbsp. gochujang
Finishing:
¼ C. chopped green onions
2 tsp. sesame seeds
Directions:
1. Ensure air fryer oven is preheated to 400 degrees.
2. Line a small pan with foil and place a rack onto the pan, then place into air fryer oven.
3. Season wings with pepper and salt and place onto the rack.
4. Set temperature to 160°F, and set time to 20 minutes and air fry 20 minutes, turning at 10 minutes.
5. As chicken air fries, mix together all the sauce components.
6. Once a thermometer says that the chicken has reached 160 degrees, take out wings and place into a bowl.
7. Pour half of the sauce mixture over wings, tossing well to coat.
8. Put coated wings back into air fryer for 5 minutes or till they reach 165 degrees.
9. Remove and sprinkle with green onions and sesame seeds. Dip into extra sauce.
PER SERVING: CALORIES: 356; FAT: 26G; PROTEIN:23G; SUGAR:2G

Almond Flour Coco-Milk Battered Chicken

Prep: 5 Minutes • Cook Time: 30 Minutes • Total: 35 Minutes
Serves: 4
Ingredients
¼ cup coconut milk
½ cup almond flour
1 ½ tablespoons old bay Cajun seasoning
1 egg, beaten
4 small chicken thighs
Salt and pepper to taste
Directions:
1. Preheat the air fryer oven for 5 minutes.
2. Mix the egg and coconut milk in a bowl.
3. Soak the chicken thighs in the beaten egg mixture.
4. In a mixing bowl, combine the almond flour, Cajun seasoning, salt and pepper.
5. Dredge the chicken thighs in the almond flour mixture.
6. Place in the air fryer basket.
7. Cook for 30 minutes at 350°F.
PER SERVING: CALORIES: 590; FAT: 38G; PROTEIN:32.5G; CARBS:3.2G

Sweet And Sour Chicken

Prep: 5 Minutes • Cook Time: 20 Minutes • Total: 25 Minutes
Serves: 6
Ingredients
3 Chicken Breasts, cubed
1/2 Cup Flour
1/2 Cup Cornstarch
2 Red Peppers, sliced
1Onion,chopped2 Carrots, julienned
3/4 Cup Sugar
2 Tbsps Cornstarch
1/3 Cup Vinegar
2/3 Cup Water
1/4 cup Soy sauce
1 Tbsp Ketchup
Directions:
1.   Preheat the air fryer oven to 375 degrees.
2.   Combine the flour, cornstarch and chicken in an air tight container and shake to combine
3.   Remove chicken from the container and shake off any excess flour.
4.   Add chicken to the Air Fryer tray and cook for 20 minutes.
5.   In a saucepan, whisk together sugar, water, vinegar, soy sauce and ketchup. Bring to a boil over medium heat, reduce the heat then simmer for 2 minutes
6.   After cooking the chicken for 20 minutes, add the vegetables and sauce mixture to the air fryer oven and cook for another 5 minutes
7.   Serve over hot rice

Basil-Garlic Breaded Chicken Bake

Prep: 5 Minutes • Cook Time: 25 Minutes • Total: 30 Minutes
Serves: 2
Ingredients
2 boneless skinless chicken breast halves (4 ounces each)
1 tablespoon butter, melted
1 large tomato, seeded and chopped
2 garlic cloves, minced
1 1/2 tablespoons minced fresh basil
1/2 tablespoon olive oil
1/2 teaspoon salt
1/4 cup all-purpose flour
1/4 cup egg substitute
1/4 cup grated Parmesan cheese
1/4 cup dry bread crumbs
1/4 teaspoon pepper
Directions:
1.   In shallow bowl, whisk well egg substitute and place flour in a separate bowl. Dip chicken in flour, then egg, and then flour. In small bowl whisk well butter, bread crumbs and cheese. Sprinkle over chicken.
2.   Lightly grease baking pan of air fryer with cooking spray. Place breaded chicken on bottom of pan. Cover with foil.
3.   For 20 minutes, cook on 390°F.
4.   Meanwhile, in a bowl whisk well remaining ingredient.
5.   Remove foil from pan and then pour over chicken the remaining Ingredients.
6.   Cook for 8 minutes.
7.   Serve and enjoy.
PER SERVING: CALORIES: 311; FAT: 11G; PROTEIN:31G; CARBS:22G

Buffalo Chicken Wings

Prep: 5 Minutes • Cook Time: 30 Minutes • Total: 35 Minutes
Serves: 8
Ingredients
1 tsp. salt
1-2 tbsp. brown sugar
1 tbsp. Worcestershire sauce
½ C. vegan butter
½ C. cayenne pepper sauce
4 pounds chicken wings
Directions:
1.   Whisk salt, brown sugar, Worcestershire sauce, butter, and hot sauce together and set to the side.
2.   Dry wings and add to air fryer basket.
3.   Set temperature to 380°F, and set time to 25 minutes. Cook tossing halfway through.
4.   When timer sounds, shake wings and bump up the temperature to 400 degrees and cook another 5 minutes.
5.   Take out wings and place into a big bowl. Add sauce and toss well.
6.   Serve alongside celery sticks.
PER SERVING: CALORIES: 402; FAT: 16G; PROTEIN:17G; SUGAR:4G

Zingy & Nutty Chicken Wings

Prep: 5 Minutes • Cook Time: 18 Minutes • Total: 23 Minutes
Serves: 4
Ingredients
1 tablespoon fish sauce
1 tablespoon fresh lemon juice
1 teaspoon sugar
12 chicken middle wings, cut into half
2 fresh lemongrass stalks, chopped finely
¼ cup unsalted cashews, crushed
Directions:
1.   In a bowl, mix together fish sauce, lime juice and sugar.
2.   Add wings ad coat with mixture generously. Refrigerate to marinate for about 1-2 hours.
3.   Preheat the air fryer oven to 355 degrees F.
4.   In the air fryer oven pan, place lemongrass stalks. Cook for about 2-3 minutes. Remove the cashew mixture from Air fryer and transfer into a bowl. Now, set the air fryer oven to 390 degrees F.
5.   Place the chicken wings in Air fryer pan. Cook for about 13-15 minutes further.
6.   Transfer the wings into serving plates. Sprinkle with cashew mixture and serve.

Honey and Wine Chicken Breasts

Prep: 5 Minutes • Cook Time: 15 Minutes • Total: 20 Minutes
Serves: 4
Ingredients
2 chicken breasts, rinsed and halved
1 tablespoon melted butter
1/2 teaspoon freshly ground pepper, or to taste
3/4 teaspoon sea salt, or to taste
1 teaspoon paprika
1 teaspoon dried rosemary
2 tablespoons dry white wine
1 tablespoon honey
Directions:
1.   Firstly, pat the chicken breasts dry. Lightly coat them with the melted butter.
2.   Then, add the remaining ingredients.
3.   Transfer them to the air fryer basket; bake about 15 minutes at 330 degrees F. Serve warm and enjoy!
PER SERVING: CALORIES: 189; FAT: 14G; PROTEIN:11G; SUGAR:1G

Chicken Fillets, Brie & Ham

Prep: 5 Minutes • Cook Time: 15 Minutes • Total: 20 Minutes
Serves: 4
Ingredients
2 Large Chicken Fillets
Freshly Ground Black Pepper
4 Small Slices of Brie (Or your cheese of choice)
1 Tbsp Freshly Chopped Chives
4 Slices Cured Ham
Directions:
1.   Slice the fillets into four and make incisions as you would for a hamburger bun. Leave a little "hinge" uncut at the back. Season the inside and pop some brie and chives in there. Close them, and wrap them each in a slice of ham. Brush with oil and pop them into the basket.
2.   Heat your fryer to 350° F. Pour into the Oven rack/basket. Place the Rack on the middle-shelf of the Air fryer oven. Set temperature to 400°F, and set time to 15 minutes. Roast the little parcels until they look tasty (15 min)

Chicken Fajitas

Prep: 10 Minutes • Cook Time: 10 Minutes • Total: 20 Minutes
Serves: 4
Ingredients
4 boneless, skinless chicken breasts, sliced
1 small red onion, sliced
2 red bell peppers, sliced
½ cup spicy ranch salad dressing, divided
½ teaspoon dried oregano
8 corn tortillas
2 cups torn butter lettuce
2 avocados, peeled and chopped
Directions:
1.   Place the chicken, onion, and pepper in the air fryer basket. Drizzle with 1 tablespoon of the salad dressing and add the oregano. Toss to combine.
2.   Place the Rack on the middle-shelf of the Air fryer oven. Set temperature to 165°F, and set time to 14 minutes. Grill for 10 to 14 minutes or until the chicken is 165°F on a food thermometer. Transfer the chicken and vegetables to a bowl and toss with the remaining salad dressing. Serve the chicken mixture with the tortillas, lettuce, and avocados and let everyone make their own creations.
PER SERVING: CALORIES: 783; FAT: 38G; PROTEIN:72; FIBER:12G

Crispy Honey Garlic Chicken Wings

Prep: 10 Minutes • Cook Time: 25 Minutes • Total: 35 Minutes
Serves: 8
Ingredients
1/8 C. water
½ tsp. salt
4 tbsp. minced garlic
¼ C. vegan butter
¼ C. raw honey
¾ C. almond flour
16 chicken wings
Directions:
1.   Rinse off and dry chicken wings well.
2.   Spray air fryer basket with olive oil.
3.   Coat chicken wings with almond flour and add coated wings to air fryer.
4.   Pour into the Oven basket. Place the basket on the middle-shelf of the Air fryer oven. Set temperature to 380°F, and set time to 25 minutes. Cook shaking every 5 minutes.
5.   When the timer goes off, cook 5-10 minutes at 400 degrees till skin becomes crispy and dry.
6.   As chicken cooks, melt butter in a saucepan and add garlic. Sauté garlic 5 minutes. Add salt and honey, simmering 20 minutes. Make sure to stir every so often, so the sauce does not burn. Add a bit of water after 15 minutes to ensure sauce does not harden.
7.   Take out chicken wings from air fryer and coat in sauce. Enjoy!
PER SERVING: CALORIES: 435; FAT: 19G; PROTEIN:31G; SUGAR:6G

BBQ Chicken Recipe from Greece

Prep: 10 Minutes • Cook Time: 25 Minutes • Total: 35 Minutes
Serves: 4
Ingredients
1 (8 ounce) container fat-free plain yogurt
2 tablespoons fresh lemon juice
2 teaspoons dried oregano
1-pound skinless, boneless chicken breast halves - cut into 1-inch pieces
1 large red onion, cut into wedges
1/2 teaspoon lemon zest
1/2 teaspoon salt
1 large green bell pepper, cut into 1 1/2-inch pieces
1/3 cup crumbled feta cheese with basil and sun-dried tomatoes
1/4 teaspoon ground black pepper
1/4 teaspoon crushed dried rosemary
Directions:
1.   In a shallow dish, mix well rosemary, pepper, salt, oregano, lemon juice, lemon zest, feta cheese, and yogurt. Add chicken and toss well to coat. Marinate in the ref for 3 hours.
2.   Thread bell pepper, onion, and chicken pieces in skewers. Place on skewer rack.
3.   For 12 minutes, cook on 360°F. Halfway through cooking time, turnover skewers. If needed, cook in batches.
4.   Serve and enjoy.
PER SERVING: CALORIES: 242; FAT: 7.5G; PROTEIN:31G; SUGAR:6G

Lemon-Pepper Chicken Wings

Prep: 10 Minutes • Cook Time: 20 Minutes • Total: 30 Minutes
Serves: 4
Ingredients
8 whole chicken wings
Juice of ½ lemon
½ teaspoon garlic powder
1 teaspoon onion powder
Salt
Pepper
¼ cup low-fat buttermilk
½ cup all-purpose flour
Cooking oil

Directions:
1.   Place the wings in a sealable plastic bag. Drizzle the wings with the lemon juice. Season the wings with the garlic powder, onion powder, and salt and pepper to taste.
2.   Seal the bag. Shake thoroughly to combine the seasonings and coat the wings.
3.   Pour the buttermilk and the flour into separate bowls large enough to dip the wings.
4.   Spray the air fryer oven basket with cooking oil.
5.   One at a time, dip the wings in the buttermilk and then the flour.
6.   Place the wings in the air fryer oven basket. It is okay to stack them on top of each other. Spray the wings with cooking oil, being sure to spray the bottom layer. Set temperature to 360°F and cook for 5 minutes.
7.   Remove the basket and shake it to ensure all of the pieces will cook fully.
8.   Return the basket to the air fryer oven and continue to cook the chicken. Repeat shaking every 5 minutes until a total of 20 minutes has passed.
9.   Cool before serving.
PER SERVING: CALORIES: 347; FAT: 12G; PROTEIN:46G; FIBER:1G

Cheesy Chicken in Leek-Tomato Sauce

Prep: 10 Minutes • Cook Time: 20 Minutes • Total: 30 Minutes
Serves: 4
Ingredients
2 large-sized chicken breasts, cut in half lengthwise
Salt and ground black pepper, to taste
4 ounces Cheddar cheese, cut into sticks
1 tablespoon sesame oil
1 cup leeks, chopped
2 cloves garlic, minced
2/3 cup roasted vegetable stock
2/3 cup tomato puree
1 teaspoon dried rosemary
1 teaspoon dried thyme

Directions:
1.   Firstly, season chicken breasts with the salt and black pepper; place a piece of Cheddar cheese in the middle. Then, tie it using a kitchen string; drizzle with sesame oil and reserve.
2.   Add the leeks and garlic to the oven safe bowl.
3.   Cook in the air fryer oven at 390 degrees F for 5 minutes or until tender.
4.   Add the reserved chicken. Throw in the other ingredients and cook for 12 to 13 minutes more or until the chicken is done. Enjoy.

Mexican Chicken Burgers

Prep: 10 Minutes • Cook Time: 10 Minutes • Total: 20 Minutes
Serves: 6
Ingredients
1 jalapeno pepper
1 tsp. cayenne pepper
1 tbsp. mustard powder
1 tbsp. oregano
1 tbsp. thyme
3 tbsp. smoked paprika
1 beaten egg
1 small head of cauliflower
4 chicken breasts
Directions:
1.   Ensure your air fryer oven is preheated to 350 degrees.
2.   Add seasonings to a blender. Slice cauliflower into florets and add to blender.
3.   Pulse till mixture resembles that of breadcrumbs.
4.   Take out ¾ of cauliflower mixture and add to a bowl. Set to the side. In another bowl, beat your egg and set to the side.
5.   Remove skin and bones from chicken breasts and add to blender with remaining cauliflower mixture. Season with pepper and salt.
6.   Take out mixture and form into burger shapes. Roll each patty in cauliflower crumbs, then the egg, and back into crumbs again.
7.   Place coated patties into the Oven rack/basket. Place the Rack on the middle-shelf of the Air fryer oven. Set temperature to 350°F, and set time to 10 minutes.
8.   Flip over at 10-minute mark. They are done when crispy.
PER SERVING: CALORIES: 234; FAT: 18G; PROTEIN:24G; SUGAR:1G

Caesar Marinated Grilled Chicken

Prep: 10 Minutes • Cook Time: 24 Minutes • Total: 34 Minutes
Serves: 3
Ingredients
¼ cup crouton
1 teaspoon lemon zest. Form into ovals, skewer and grill.
1/2 cup Parmesan
1/4 cup breadcrumbs
1-pound ground chicken
2 tablespoons Caesar dressing and more for drizzling
2-4 romaine leaves
Directions:
1.   In a shallow dish, mix well chicken, 2 tablespoons Caesar dressing, parmesan, and breadcrumbs. Mix well with hands. Form into 1-inch oval patties.
2.   Thread chicken pieces in skewers. Place on skewer rack in air fryer oven.
3.   For 12 minutes, cook on 360°F. Halfway through cooking time, turnover skewers. If needed, cook in batches.
4.   Serve and enjoy on a bed of lettuce and sprinkle with croutons and extra dressing.
PER SERVING: CALORIES: 339; FAT: 18.9G; PROTEIN:32.6G; SUGAR:1G

Fried Chicken Livers

Prep: 5 Minutes • Cook Time: 10 Minutes • Total: 15 Minutes
Serves: 4

Ingredients
1 pound chicken livers
1 cup flour
1/2 cup cornmeal
2 teaspoons your favorite seasoning blend
3 eggs
2 tablespoons milk

Directions:
1. Clean and rinse the livers, pat dry.
2. Beat eggs in a shallow bowl and mix in milk.
3. In another bowl combine flour, cornmeal, and seasoning, mixing until even.
4. Dip the livers in the egg mix, then toss them in the flour mix.
5. Pour into the Oven rack/basket. Place the Rack on the middle-shelf of the Air fryer oven. Set temperature to 375°F, and set time to 10 minutes. Toss at least once halfway through.

PER SERVING: CALORIES: 409; FAT: 11G; PROTEIN:36G; FIBER:2G

Crispy Southern Fried Chicken

Prep: 10 Minutes • Cook Time: 25 Minutes • Total: 35 Minutes
Serves: 4

Ingredients
1 tsp. cayenne pepper
2 tbsp. mustard powder
2 tbsp. oregano
2 tbsp. thyme
3 tbsp. coconut milk
1 beaten egg
¼ C. cauliflower
¼ C. gluten-free oats
8 chicken drumsticks

Directions:
1. Ensure the air fryer oven is preheated to 350 degrees.
2. Lay out chicken and season with pepper and salt on all sides.
3. Add all other ingredients to a blender, blending till a smooth-like breadcrumb mixture is created. Place in a bowl and add a beaten egg to another bowl.
4. Dip chicken into breadcrumbs, then into egg, and breadcrumbs once more.
5. Place coated drumsticks into the air fryer basket. Set temperature to 350°F, and set time to 20 minutes and cook 20 minutes. Bump up the temperature to 390 degrees and cook another 5 minutes till crispy.

PER SERVING: CALORIES: 504; FAT: 18G; PROTEIN:35G; SUGAR:5G

Chicken Roast with Pineapple Salsa

Prep: 10 Minutes • Cook Time: 45 Minutes • Total: 55 Minutes
Serves: 2

Ingredients

¼ cup extra virgin olive oil
¼ cup freshly chopped cilantro
1 avocado, diced
1-pound boneless chicken breasts
2 cups canned pineapples
2 teaspoons honey
Juice from 1 lime
Salt and pepper to taste

Directions:

1. Preheat the air fryer oven to 390°F.
2. Place the grill pan accessory in the air fryer.
3. Season the chicken breasts with lime juice, olive oil, honey, salt, and pepper.
4. Place on the grill pan and cook for 45 minutes.
5. Flip the chicken every 10 minutes to grill all sides evenly.
6. Once the chicken is cooked, serve with pineapples, cilantro, and avocado.

PER SERVING: CALORIES: 744; FAT: 32.8G; PROTEIN:4.7G; SUGAR:5G

Tex-Mex Turkey Burgers

Prep: 10 Minutes • Cook Time: 15 Minutes • Total: 25 Minutes
Serves: 4

Ingredients

⅓ cup finely crushed corn tortilla chips
1 egg, beaten
¼ cup salsa
⅓ cup shredded pepper Jack cheese
Pinch salt
Freshly ground black pepper
1 pound ground turkey
1 tablespoon olive oil
1 teaspoon paprika

Directions:

1. In a medium bowl, combine the tortilla chips, egg, salsa, cheese, salt, and pepper, and mix well.
2. Add the turkey and mix gently but thoroughly with clean hands.
3. Form the meat mixture into patties about ½ inch thick. Make an indentation in the center of each patty with your thumb so the burgers don't puff up while cooking.
4. Brush the patties on both sides with the olive oil and sprinkle with paprika.
5. Pour into the Oven rack/basket. Place the Rack on the middle-shelf of the Air fryer oven. Set temperature to 165°F, and set time to 14 minutes. Grill for 14 to 16 minutes or until the meat registers at least 165°F.

PER SERVING: CALORIES: 354; FAT: 21G; PROTEIN:36G; FIBER:2G

Air Fryer Turkey Breast

Prep: 5 Minutes • Cook Time: 60 Minutes • Total: 65 Minutes
Serves: 6
Ingredients
Pepper and salt
1 oven-ready turkey breast
Turkey seasonings of choice
Directions:
1.   Preheat the air fryer to 350 degrees.
2.   Season turkey with pepper, salt, and other desired seasonings.
3.   Place turkey in air fryer basket.
4.   Pour into the Oven rack/basket. Place the Rack on the middle-shelf of the Air fryer oven. Set temperature to 350°F, and set time to 60 minutes. Cook 60 minutes. The meat should be at 165 degrees when done.
5.   Allow to rest 10-15 minutes before slicing. Enjoy.
PER SERVING: CALORIES: 212; FAT: 12G; PROTEIN:24G; SUGAR:0G

Cheese Stuffed Chicken

Prep: 5 Minutes • Cook Time: 30 Minutes • Total: 35 Minutes
Serves: 4
Ingredients
1 tablespoon creole seasoning
1 tablespoon olive oil
1 teaspoon garlic powder
1 teaspoon onion powder
4 chicken breasts, butterflied and pounded
4 slices Colby cheese
4 slices pepper jack cheese
Directions:
1.   Preheat the air fryer oven to 390°F.
2.   Place the grill pan accessory in the air fryer.
3.   Create the dry rub by mixing in a bowl the creole seasoning, garlic powder, and onion powder. Season with salt and pepper if desired.
4.   Rub the seasoning on to the chicken.
5.   Place the chicken on a working surface and place a slice each of pepper jack and Colby cheese.
6.   Fold the chicken and secure the edges with toothpicks.
7.   Brush chicken with olive oil.
8.   Grill for 30 minutes and make sure to flip the meat every 10 minutes.
PER SERVING: CALORIES: 27; FAT: 45.9G; PROTEIN:73.1G; SUGAR:0G

Orange Curried Chicken Stir-Fry

Prep: 10 Minutes • Cook Time: 18 Minutes • Total: 28 Minutes
Serves: 4
Ingredients
¾ pound boneless, skinless chicken thighs, cut into 1-inch pieces
1 yellow bell pepper, cut into 1½-inch pieces
1 small red onion, sliced
Olive oil for misting
¼ cup chicken stock
2 tablespoons honey
¼ cup orange juice
1 tablespoon cornstarch
to 3 teaspoons curry powder

Directions:
1.   Put the chicken thighs, pepper, and red onion in the air fryer basket and mist with olive oil.
2.   Cook for 12 to 14 minutes or until the chicken is cooked to 165°F, shaking the basket halfway through cooking time.
3.   Remove the chicken and vegetables from the air fryer basket and set aside.
4.   In a 6-inch metal bowl, combine the stock, honey, orange juice, cornstarch, and curry powder, and mix well. Add the chicken and vegetables, stir, and put the bowl in the basket.
5.   Return the basket to the air fryer oven and cook for 2 minutes. Remove and stir, then cook for 2 to 3 minutes or until the sauce is thickened and bubbly.

PER SERVING: CALORIES: 230; FAT: 7G; PROTEIN:26G; FIBER:2G

Mustard Chicken Tenders

Prep: 5 Minutes • Cook Time: 20 Minutes • Total: 25 Minutes
Serves: 4
Ingredients
½ C. coconut flour
1 tbsp. spicy brown mustard
2 beaten eggs
1 pound of chicken tenders

Directions:
1.   Season tenders with pepper and salt.
2.   Place a thin layer of mustard onto tenders and then dredge in flour and dip in egg.
3.   Pour into the Oven rack/basket. Place the Rack on the middle-shelf of the Air fryer oven. Set temperature to 390°F, and set time to 20 minutes.

PER SERVING: CALORIES: 403; FAT: 20G; PROTEIN:22G; SUGAR:4G

Chicken Pot Pie with Coconut Milk

Prep: 5 Minutes • Cook Time: 30 Minutes • Total: 40 Minutes
Serves: 8
Ingredients
¼ small onion, chopped
½ cup broccoli, chopped
¾ cup coconut milk
1 cup chicken broth
1/3 cup coconut flour
1-pound ground chicken
2 cloves of garlic, minced
2 tablespoons butter
4 ½ tablespoons butter, melted
4 eggs
Salt and pepper to taste

Directions:
1. Preheat the air fryer oven for 5 minutes.
2. Place 2 tablespoons butter, broccoli, onion, garlic, coconut milk, chicken broth, and ground chicken in a baking dish that will fit in the air fryer. Season with salt and pepper to taste.
3. In a mixing bowl, combine the butter, coconut flour, and eggs.
4. Sprinkle evenly the top of the chicken and broccoli mixture with the coconut flour dough.
5. Pour into the Oven rack/basket. Place the Rack on the middle-shelf of the Air fryer oven. Set temperature to 325°F, and set time to 30 minutes.

PER SERVING: CALORIES: 366; FAT: 29.5G; PROTEIN:21.8G; SUGAR:4G

Chicken Nuggets

Prep: 10 Minutes • Cook Time: 20 Minutes • Total: 30 Minutes
Serves: 4
Ingredients
1 pound boneless, skinless chicken breasts
Chicken seasoning or rub
Salt
Pepper
2 eggs
6 tablespoons bread crumbs
2 tablespoons panko bread crumbs
Cooking oil

Directions:
1. Cut the chicken breasts into 1-inch pieces.
2. In a large bowl, combine the chicken pieces with chicken seasoning, salt, and pepper to taste.
3. In a small bowl, beat the eggs. In another bowl, combine the bread crumbs and panko.
4. Dip the chicken pieces in the eggs and then the bread crumbs.
5. Place the nuggets in the air fryer oven. Do not overcrowd the basket. Cook in batches. Spray the nuggets with cooking oil. Set temperature to 390°F and cook for 4 minutes. Open the air fryer oven and shake the basket. Cook for an additional 4 minutes. Remove the cooked nuggets from the air fryer, then repeat for the remaining chicken nuggets. Cool before serving.

PER SERVING: CALORIES: 206; FAT: 5G; PROTEIN:31G; FIBER:1G

Cheesy Chicken Fritters

Prep: 5 Minutes • Cook Time: 20 Minutes • Total: 25 Minutes
Serves: 17 Fritters
Ingredients
Chicken Fritters:
½ tsp. salt
1/8 tsp. pepper
1 ½ tbsp. fresh dill
1 1/3 C. shredded mozzarella cheese
1/3 C. coconut flour
1/3 C. vegan mayo
2 eggs
1 ½ pounds chicken breasts
Garlic Dip:
1/8 tsp. pepper
¼ tsp. salt
½ tbsp. lemon juice
1 pressed garlic cloves
1/3 C. vegan mayo
Directions:
1.   Slice chicken breasts into 1/3" pieces and place in a bowl. Add all remaining fritter ingredients to the bowl and stir well. Cover and chill 2 hours or overnight.
2.   Ensure your air fryer is preheated to 350 degrees. Spray basket with a bit of olive oil.
3.   Add marinated chicken to air fryer oven. Set temperature to 350°F, and set time to 20 minutes and cook 20 minutes, making sure to turn halfway through cooking process.
4.   To make the dipping sauce, combine all the dip ingredients until smooth.
PER SERVING: CALORIES: 467; FAT: 27G; PROTEIN:21G; SUGAR:3G

Chicken BBQ with Sweet And Sour Sauce

Prep: 5 Minutes • Cook Time: 40 Minutes • Total: 45 Minutes
Serves: 6
Ingredients
¼ cup minced garlic
¼ cup tomato paste
¾ cup minced onion
¾ cup sugar
1 cup soy sauce
1 cup water
1 cup white vinegar
6 chicken drumsticks
Salt and pepper to taste
Directions:
1.   Place all Ingredients in a Ziploc bag
2.   Allow to marinate for at least 2 hours in the fridge.
3.   Preheat the air fryer oven to 390°F.
4.   Place the grill pan accessory in the air fryer.
5.   Pour into the Oven rack/basket. Place the Rack on the middle-shelf of the Air fryer oven. Set temperature to 390°F, and set time to 40 minutes. Grill the chicken for 40 minutes.
6.   Flip the chicken every 10 minutes for even grilling.
7.   Meanwhile, pour the marinade in a saucepan and heat over medium flame until the sauce thickens.
8.   Before serving the chicken, brush with the glaze.
PER SERVING: CALORIES: 4607; FAT: 19.7G; PROTEIN:27.8G; SUGAR:3G

Thai Basil Chicken

Prep: 5 Minutes • Cook Time: 20 Minutes • Total: 25 Minutes
Serves: 4
Ingredients
4 Chicken Breasts
1 Onion
2 Bell Peppers
2 Hot Peppers
1 Tbsp Olive Oil
3 Tbsps Fish Sauce
2 Tbsps Oyster Sauce
3 Tbsps Sweet Chili Sauce
1 Tbsp Soy Sauce
1 Quart Chicken Broth
1 Tbsp Garlic Powder
1 Tbsp Chili Powder
1 Cup Thai Basil
Directions:
1.   Wash the breasts and boil them in the chicken broth for 10 minutes, then lower to simmer for another 10 minutes until tender. Take them out of the broth and allow to cool
2.   Using two forks, tear the chicken into shreds. Toss the shreds with the garlic powder, chili powder, and salt and pepper to taste
3.   Preheat the air fryer oven to 390 degrees and cook the chicken shreds for 20 minutes, at which point they will get dark brown and crispy. They will soften up as they absorb the juices from cooking with the veggies
4.   While the chicken is cooking, cut the onions and peppers into thin slices. Add the olive oil to a wok and heat for a minute on medium high heat. Toss in all the veggies and sauté for 5 minutes
5.   Add in the fish sauce, oyster sauce, soy sauce, sweet chili sauce, and stir well for 1 minute. Add the chicken and basil leaves and stir until the leaves have wilted
6.   Serve over jasmine rice.
PER SERVING: CALORIES: 351; FAT: 14G; PROTEIN:23G; SUGAR:2G

Crusted Chicken Tenders

Prep: 5 Minutes • Cook Time: 15 Minutes • Total: 20 Minutes
Serves: 3
Ingredients
½ cup all-purpose flour
2 eggs, beaten
½ cup seasoned breadcrumbs
Salt and freshly ground black pepper, to taste
2 tablespoons olive oil
¾ pound chicken tenders
Directions:
1.   In a bowl, place the flour.
2.   In a second bowl, place the eggs.
3.   In a third bowl, mix together breadcrumbs, salt, black pepper and oil.
4.   Coat the chicken tenders in the flour,
5.   Then dip into the eggs and finally coat with the breadcrumbs mixture evenly.
6.   Preheat the air fryer oven to 330 degrees F. Arrange the chicken tenderloins in Air fryer basket. Cook for about 10 minutes.
7.   Now, set the Air fryer to 390 degrees F.
8.   Cook for about 5 minutes further.

Air Fryer Chicken Parmesan

Prep: 5 Minutes • Cook Time: 9 Minutes • Total: 20 Minutes
Serves: 4
Ingredients
½ C. keto marinara
6 tbsp. mozzarella cheese
1 tbsp. melted ghee
2 tbsp. grated parmesan cheese
6 tbsp. gluten-free seasoned breadcrumbs
8-ounce chicken breasts
Directions:
1.   Ensure air fryer is preheated to 360 degrees. Spray the basket with olive oil.
2.   Mix parmesan cheese and breadcrumbs together. Melt ghee.
3.   Brush melted ghee onto the chicken and dip into breadcrumb mixture.
4.   Place coated chicken in the air fryer and top with olive oil.
5.   Pour into the Oven rack/basket. Place the Rack on the middle-shelf of the Air fryer oven. Set temperature to 360°F, and set time to 6 minutes. Cook 2 breasts for 6 minutes and top each breast with a tablespoon of sauce and 1½ tablespoons of mozzarella cheese. Cook another 3 minutes to melt cheese.
6.   Keep cooked pieces warm as you repeat the process with remaining breasts.
PER SERVING: CALORIES: 251; FAT: 10G; PROTEIN:31G; SUGAR:0G

Chicken BBQ Recipe from Peru

Prep: 5 Minutes • Cook Time: 40 Minutes • Total: 45 Minutes
Serves: 4
Ingredients
½ teaspoon dried oregano
1 teaspoon paprika
1/3 cup soy sauce
2 ½ pounds chicken, quartered
2 tablespoons fresh lime juice
2 teaspoons ground cumin
5 cloves of garlic, minced
Directions:
1.   Place all Ingredients in a Ziploc bag and shake to mix everything.
2.   Allow to marinate for at least 2 hours in the fridge.
3.   Preheat the air fryer oven to 390°F.
4.   Place the grill pan accessory in the air fryer.
5.   Grill the chicken for 40 minutes making sure to flip the chicken every 10 minutes for even grilling.
PER SERVING: CALORIES: 377; FAT: 11.8G; PROTEIN:59.7G; SUGAR:0G

Ricotta and Parsley Stuffed Turkey Breasts

Prep: 5 Minutes • Cook Time: 25 Minutes • Total: 30 Minutes
Serves: 4
Ingredients
1 turkey breast, quartered
1 cup Ricotta cheese
1/4 cup fresh Italian parsley, chopped
1 teaspoon garlic powder
1/2 teaspoon cumin powder
1 egg, beaten
1 teaspoon paprika
Salt and ground black pepper, to taste
Crushed tortilla chips
1 ½ tablespoons extra-virgin olive oil

Directions:
1. Firstly, flatten out each piece of turkey breast with a rolling pin. Prepare three mixing bowls.
2. In a shallow bowl, combine Ricotta cheese with the parsley, garlic powder, and cumin powder.
3. Place the Ricotta/parsley mixture in the middle of each piece. Repeat with the remaining pieces of the turkey breast and roll them up.
4. In another shallow bowl, whisk the egg together with paprika. In the third shallow bowl, combine the salt, pepper, and crushed tortilla chips.
5. Dip each roll in the whisked egg, then, roll them over the tortilla chips mixture.
6. Transfer prepared rolls to the air fryer basket. Drizzle olive oil over all.
7. Cook at 350 degrees F for 25 minutes, working in batches. Serve warm, garnished with some extra parsley, if desired.

Cheesy Turkey-Rice with Broccoli

Prep: 5 Minutes • Cook Time: 40 Minutes • Total: 45 Minutes
Serves: 4
Ingredients
1 cup cooked, chopped turkey meat
1 tablespoon and 1-1/2 teaspoons butter, melted
1/2 (10 ounce) package frozen broccoli, thawed
1/2 (7 ounce) package whole wheat crackers, crushed
1/2 cup shredded Cheddar cheese
1/2 cup uncooked white rice

Directions:
1. Bring to a boil 2 cups of water in a saucepan. Stir in rice and simmer for 20 minutes. Turn off fire and set aside.
2. Lightly grease baking pan of air fryer with cooking spray. Mix in cooked rice, cheese, broccoli, and turkey. Toss well to mix.
3. Mix well melted butter and crushed crackers in a small bowl. Evenly spread on top of rice.
4. Pour into the Oven rack/basket. Place the Rack on the middle-shelf of the Air fryer oven. Set temperature to 360°F, and set time to 20 minutes until tops are lightly browned.
5. Serve and enjoy.
PER SERVING: CALORIES: 269; FAT: 11.8G; PROTEIN:17G; SUGAR:0G

Jerk Chicken Wings

Prep: 10 Minutes • Cook Time: 16 Minutes • Total: 26 Minutes
Serves: 6

Ingredients

1 tsp. salt
½ C. red wine vinegar
5 tbsp. lime juice
4 chopped scallions
1 tbsp. grated ginger
2 tbsp. brown sugar
1 tbsp. chopped thyme
1 tsp. white pepper
1 tsp. cayenne pepper
1 tsp. cinnamon
1 tbsp. allspice
1 Habanero pepper (seeds/ribs removed and chopped finely)
6 chopped garlic cloves
2 tbsp. low-sodium soy sauce
2 tbsp. olive oil
4 pounds of chicken wings

Directions:

1. Combine all ingredients except wings in a bowl. Pour into a gallon bag and add chicken wings. Chill 2-24 hours to marinate.
2. Ensure your air fryer oven is preheated to 390 degrees.
3. Place chicken wings into a strainer to drain excess liquids.
4. Pour half of the wings into your air fryer basket. Set temperature to 390°F, and set time to 16 minutes and cook 14-16 minutes, making sure to shake halfway through the cooking process.
5. Remove and repeat the process with remaining wings.

PER SERVING: CALORIES: 374; FAT: 14G; PROTEIN:33G; SUGAR:4G

Pork Recipes

Pork Taquitos

Prep: 10 Minutes • Cook Time: 16 Minutes • Total: 26 Minutes
Serves: 8
Ingredients
1 juiced lime
10 whole wheat tortillas
2 ½ C. shredded mozzarella cheese
30 ounces of cooked and shredded pork tenderloin
Directions:
1.   Ensure your air fryer oven is preheated to 380 degrees.
2.   Drizzle pork with lime juice and gently mix.
3.   Heat up tortillas in the microwave with a dampened paper towel to soften.
4.   Add about 3 ounces of pork and ¼ cup of shredded cheese to each tortilla. Tightly roll them up.
5.   Spray the air fryer basket with a bit of olive oil.
6.   Set temperature to 380°F, and set time to 10 minutes. Air fry taquitos 7-10 minutes till tortillas turn a slight golden color, making sure to flip halfway through cooking process.
PER SERVING: CALORIES: 309; FAT: 11G; PROTEIN:21G; SUGAR:2G

Panko-Breaded Pork Chops

Prep: 5 Minutes • Cook Time: 12 Minutes • Total: 17 Minutes
Serves: 6
Ingredients
5 (3½- to 5-ounce) pork chops (bone-in or boneless)
Seasoning salt
Pepper
¼ cup all-purpose flour
2 tablespoons panko bread crumbs
Cooking oil
Directions:
1.   Season the pork chops with the seasoning salt and pepper to taste.
2.   Sprinkle the flour on both sides of the pork chops, then coat both sides with panko bread crumbs.
3.   Place the pork chops in the air fryer. Stacking them is okay.
4.   Spray the pork chops with cooking oil. Pour into the Oven rack/basket. Place the Rack on the middle-shelf of the Air fryer oven. Set temperature to 375°F, and set time to 6 minutes. Cook for 6 minutes.
5.   Open the air fryer oven and flip the pork chops. Cook for an additional 6 minutes
6.   Cool before serving.
7.   Typically, bone-in pork chops are juicier than boneless. If you prefer really juicy pork chops, use bone-in.
PER SERVING: CALORIES: 246; FAT: 13G; PROTEIN:26G; FIBER:0G

Apricot Glazed Pork Tenderloins

Prep: 5 Minutes • Cook Time: 30 Minutes • Total: 35 Minutes
Serves: 3
Ingredients
1 teaspoon salt
1/2 teaspoon pepper
1-lb pork tenderloin
2 tablespoons minced fresh rosemary or 1 tablespoon dried rosemary, crushed
2 tablespoons olive oil, divided
garlic cloves, minced
Apricot Glaze Ingredients
1 cup apricot preserves
garlic cloves, minced
4 tablespoons lemon juice
Directions:
1.   Mix well pepper, salt, garlic, oil, and rosemary. Brush all over pork. If needed cut pork crosswise in half to fit in air fryer.
2.   Lightly grease baking pan of air fryer with cooking spray. Add pork.
3.   For 3 minutes per side, brown pork in a preheated 390°F air fryer.
4.   Meanwhile, mix well all glaze Ingredients in a small bowl. Baste pork every 5 minutes.
5.   Cook for 20 minutes at 330°F.
6.   Serve and enjoy.
PER SERVING: CALORIES: 281; FAT: 9G; PROTEIN:23G; FIBER:0G

Barbecue Flavored Pork Ribs

Prep: 5 Minutes • Cook Time: 15 Minutes • Total: 25 Minutes
Serves: 6
Ingredients
¼ cup honey, divided
¾ cup BBQ sauce
2 tablespoons tomato ketchup
1 tablespoon Worcestershire sauce
1 tablespoon soy sauce
½ teaspoon garlic powder
Freshly ground white pepper, to taste
1¾ pound pork ribs
Directions:
1.   In a large bowl, mix together 3 tablespoons of honey and remaining ingredients except pork ribs.
2.   Refrigerate to marinate for about 20 minutes.
3.   Preheat the air fryer oven to 355 degrees F.
4.   Place the ribs in an Air fryer basket.
5.   Cook for about 13 minutes.
6.   Remove the ribs from the air fryer oven and coat with remaining honey.
7.   Serve hot.

Balsamic Glazed Pork Chops

Prep: 5 Minutes • Cook Time: 50 Minutes • Total: 55 Minutes
Serves: 4
Ingredients
¾ cup balsamic vinegar
1 ½ tablespoons sugar
1 tablespoon butter
3 tablespoons olive oil
tablespoons salt
3 pork rib chops
Directions:
1.   Place all ingredients in bowl and allow the meat to marinate in the fridge for at least 2 hours.
2.   Preheat the air fryer oven to 390°F.
3.   Place the grill pan accessory in the air fryer.
4.   Grill the pork chops for 20 minutes making sure to flip the meat every 10 minutes for even grilling.
5.   Meanwhile, pour the balsamic vinegar on a saucepan and allow to simmer for at least 10 minutes until the sauce thickens.
6.   Brush the meat with the glaze before serving.
PER SERVING: CALORIES: 274; FAT: 18G; PROTEIN:17G

Rustic Pork Ribs

Prep: 5 Minutes • Cook Time: 15 Minutes • Total: 25 Minutes
Serves: 4
Ingredients
1 rack of pork ribs
3 tablespoons dry red wine
1 tablespoon soy sauce
1/2 teaspoon dried thyme
1/2 teaspoon onion powder
1/2 teaspoon garlic powder
1/2 teaspoon ground black pepper
1 teaspoon smoke salt
1 tablespoon cornstarch
1/2 teaspoon olive oil
Directions:
1.   Begin by preheating your air fryer oven to 390 degrees F. Place all ingredients in a mixing bowl and let them marinate at least 1 hour.
2.   Pour into the Oven rack/basket. Place the Rack on the middle-shelf of the Air fryer oven. Set temperature to 390°F, and set time to 25 minutes. Cook the marinated ribs approximately 25 minutes.
3.   Serve hot.

Keto Parmesan Crusted Pork Chops

Prep: 10 Minutes • Cook Time: 15 Minutes • Total: 25 Minutes
Serves: 8
Ingredients
3 tbsp. grated parmesan cheese
1 C. pork rind crumbs
2 beaten eggs
¼ tsp. chili powder
½ tsp. onion powder
1 tsp. smoked paprika
¼ tsp. pepper
½ tsp. salt
4-6 thick boneless pork chops
Directions:
1.   Ensure your air fryer oven is preheated to 400 degrees.
2.   With pepper and salt, season both sides of pork chops.
3.   In a food processor, pulse pork rinds into crumbs. Mix crumbs with other seasonings. Beat eggs and add to another bowl.
4.   Dip pork chops into eggs then into pork rind crumb mixture.
5.   Spray down air fryer with olive oil and add pork chops to the basket. Set temperature to 400°F, and set time to 15 minutes.
PER SERVING: CALORIES: 422; FAT: 19G; PROTEIN:38G; SUGAR:2G

Crispy Fried Pork Chops the Southern Way

Prep: 10 Minutes • Cook Time: 25 Minutes • Total: 35 Minutes
Serves: 4
Ingredients
½ cup all-purpose flour
½ cup low fat buttermilk
½ teaspoon black pepper
½ teaspoon Tabasco sauce
teaspoon paprika
3 bone-in pork chops
Directions:
1.   Place the buttermilk and hot sauce in a Ziploc bag and add the pork chops. Allow to marinate for at least an hour in the fridge.
2.   In a bowl, combine the flour, paprika, and black pepper.
3.   Remove pork from the Ziploc bag and dredge in the flour mixture.
4.   Preheat the air fryer oven to 390°F.
5.   Spray the pork chops with cooking oil.
6.   Pour into the Oven rack/basket. Place the Rack on the middle-shelf of the Air fryer oven. Set temperature to 390°F, and set time to 25 minutes.
PER SERVING: CALORIES: 427; FAT: 21.2G; PROTEIN:46.4G; SUGAR:2G

Fried Pork Quesadilla

Prep: 10 Minutes • Cook Time: 12 Minutes • Total: 22 Minutes
Serves: 2
Ingredients
Two 6-inch corn or flour tortilla shells
1 medium-sized pork shoulder, approximately 4 ounces, sliced
½ medium-sized white onion, sliced
½ medium-sized red pepper, sliced
½ medium sized green pepper, sliced
½ medium sized yellow pepper, sliced
¼ cup of shredded pepper-jack cheese
¼ cup of shredded mozzarella cheese
Directions:
1. Preheat the air fryer oven to 350 degrees.
2. In the oven on high heat for 20 minutes, grill the pork, onion, and peppers in foil in the same pan, allowing the moisture from the vegetables and the juice from the pork mingle together. Remove pork and vegetables in foil from the oven. While they're cooling, sprinkle half the shredded cheese over one of the tortillas, then cover with the pieces of pork, onions, and peppers, and then layer on the rest of the shredded cheese. Top with the second tortilla. Place directly on hot surface of the air fryer basket.
3. Set the air fryer timer for 6 minutes. After 6 minutes, when the air fryer shuts off, flip the tortillas onto the other side with a spatula; the cheese should be melted enough that it won't fall apart, but be careful anyway not to spill any toppings!
4. Reset the air fryer to 350 degrees for another 6 minutes.
5. After 6 minutes, when the air fryer shuts off, the tortillas should be browned and crisp, and the pork, onion, peppers and cheese will be crispy and hot and delicious. Remove with tongs and let sit on a serving plate to cool for a few minutes before slicing.

Cilantro-Mint Pork BBQ Thai Style

Prep: 5 Minutes • Cook Time: 15 Minutes • Total: 20 Minutes
Serves: 3
Ingredients
1 minced hot chile
1 minced shallot
1-pound ground pork
2 tablespoons fish sauce
2 tablespoons lime juice
3 tablespoons basil
tablespoons chopped mint
3 tablespoons cilantro
Directions:
1. In a shallow dish, mix well all Ingredients with hands. Form into 1-inch ovals.
2. Thread ovals in skewers. Place on skewer rack in air fryer.
3. For 15 minutes, cook on 360°F. Halfway through cooking time, turnover skewers. If needed, cook in batches.
4. Serve and enjoy.
PER SERVING: CALORIES: 455; FAT: 31.5G; PROTEIN:40.4G

Tuscan Pork Chops

Prep: 10 Minutes • Cook Time: 10 Minutes • Total: 20 Minutes
Serves: 4
Ingredients
1/4 cup all-purpose flour
1 teaspoon salt
3/4 teaspoons seasoned pepper
4 (1-inch-thick) boneless pork chops
1 tablespoon olive oil
3 to 4 garlic cloves
1/3 cup balsamic vinegar
1/3 cup chicken broth
3 plum tomatoes, seeded and diced
tablespoons capers
Directions:
1. Combine flour, salt, and pepper
2. Press pork chops into flour mixture on both sides until evenly covered.
3. Cook in your air fryer oven at 360 degrees for 14 minutes, flipping half way through.
4. While the pork chops cook, warm olive oil in a medium skillet.
5. Add garlic and sauté for 1 minute; then mix in vinegar and chicken broth.
6. Add capers and tomatoes and turn to high heat.
7. Bring the sauce to a boil, stirring regularly, then add pork chops, cooking for one minute.
8. Remove from heat and cover for about 5 minutes to allow the pork to absorb some of the sauce; serve hot.
PER SERVING: CALORIES: 349; FAT: 23G; PROTEIN:20G; FIBER:1.5G

Italian Parmesan Breaded Pork Chops

Prep: 5 Minutes • Cook Time: 25 Minutes • Total: 30 Minutes
Serves: 5
Ingredients
5 (3½- to 5-ounce) pork chops (bone-in or boneless)
1 teaspoon Italian seasoning
Seasoning salt
Pepper
¼ cup all-purpose flour
2 tablespoons Italian bread crumbs
3 tablespoons finely grated Parmesan cheese
Cooking oil
Directions:
1. Season the pork chops with the Italian seasoning and seasoning salt and pepper to taste.
2. Sprinkle the flour on both sides of the pork chops, then coat both sides with the bread crumbs and Parmesan cheese.
3. Place the pork chops in the air fryer basket. Stacking them is okay. Spray the pork chops with cooking oil. Set temperature to 390°F and cook for 6 minutes.
4. Open the air fryer and flip the pork chops. Cook for an additional 6 minutes.
5. Cool before serving. Instead of seasoning salt, you can use either chicken or pork rub for additional flavor. You can find these rubs in the spice aisle of the grocery store.
PER SERVING: CALORIES: 334; FAT: 7G; PROTEIN:34G; FIBER:0G

Crispy Roast Garlic-Salt Pork

Prep: 5 Minutes • Cook Time: 45 Minutes • Total: 50 Minutes
Serves: 4
Ingredients
1 teaspoon Chinese five spice powder
1 teaspoon white pepper
2 pounds pork belly
2 teaspoons garlic salt
Directions:
1.   Preheat the air fryer oven to 390°F.
2.   Mix all the spices in a bowl to create the dry rub.
3.   Score the skin of the pork belly with a knife and season the entire pork with the spice rub.
4.   Place in the air fryer basket and cook for 40 to 45 minutes until the skin is crispy.
5.   Chop before serving.
PER SERVING: CALORIES: 785; FAT:80.7G; PROTEIN:14.2G; FIBER:0G

Crispy Breaded Pork Chops

Prep: 10 Minutes • Cook Time: 15 Minutes • Total: 25 Minutes
Serves: 8
Ingredients
1/8 tsp. pepper
¼ tsp. chili powder
½ tsp. onion powder
½ tsp. garlic powder
1 ¼ tsp. sweet paprika
2 tbsp. grated parmesan cheese
1/3 C. crushed cornflake crumbs
½ C. panko breadcrumbs
1 beaten egg
6 center-cut boneless pork chops
Directions:
1.   Ensure that your air fryer is preheated to 400 degrees. Spray the basket with olive oil.
2.   With ½ teaspoon salt and pepper, season both sides of pork chops.
3.   Combine ¾ teaspoon salt with pepper, chili powder, onion powder, garlic powder, paprika, cornflake crumbs, panko breadcrumbs and parmesan cheese.
4.   Beat egg in another bowl.
5.   Dip pork chops into the egg and then crumb mixture.
6.   Add pork chops to air fryer and spritz with olive oil.
7.   Pour into the Oven rack/basket. Place the Rack on the middle-shelf of the Air fryer oven. Set temperature to 400°F, and set time to 12 minutes.Cook 12 minutes, making sure to flip over halfway through cooking process.
8.   Only add 3 chops in at a time and repeat the process with remaining pork chops.
PER SERVING: CALORIES: 378; FAT: 13G; PROTEIN:33G; SUGAR:1G

Ginger, Garlic And Pork Dumplings

Prep: 10 Minutes • Cook Time: 15 Minutes • Total: 25 Minutes
Serves: 8
Ingredients
¼ teaspoon crushed red pepper
½ teaspoon sugar
1 tablespoon chopped fresh ginger
1 tablespoon chopped garlic
1 teaspoon canola oil
1 teaspoon toasted sesame oil
18 dumpling wrappers
2 tablespoons rice vinegar
2 teaspoons soy sauce
4 cups bok choy, chopped
4 ounces ground pork
Directions:
1.	Heat oil in a skillet and sauté the ginger and garlic until fragrant. Stir in the ground pork and cook for 5 minutes.
2.	Stir in the bok choy and crushed red pepper. Season with salt and pepper to taste. Allow to cool.
3.	Place the meat mixture in the middle of the dumpling wrappers. Fold the wrappers to seal the meat mixture in.
4.	Place the bok choy in the grill pan.
5.	Cook the dumplings in the air fryer at 330°F for 15 minutes.
6.	Meanwhile, prepare the dipping sauce by combining the remaining Ingredients in a bowl.
PER SERVING: CALORIES: 137; FAT: 5G; PROTEIN:7G

Caramelized Pork Shoulder

Prep: 10 Minutes • Cook Time: 20 Minutes • Total: 30 Minutes
Serves: 8
Ingredients
1/3 cup soy sauce
2 tablespoons sugar
1 tablespoon honey
2 pound pork shoulder, cut into 1½-inch thick slices
Directions:
1.	In a bowl, mix together all ingredients except pork.
2.	Add pork and coat with marinade generously.
3.	Cover and refrigerate o marinate for about 2-8 hours.
4.	Preheat the air fryer oven to 335 degrees F.
5.	Place the pork in an Air fryer basket.
6.	Cook for about 10 minutes.
7.	Now, set the air fryer oven to 390 degrees F. Cook for about 10 minutes

Curry Pork Roast in Coconut Sauce

Prep: 10 Minutes • Cook Time: 60 Minutes • Total: 70 Minutes
Serves: 6
Ingredients
½ teaspoon curry powder
½ teaspoon ground turmeric powder
1 can unsweetened coconut milk
1 tablespoons sugar
2 tablespoons fish sauce
2 tablespoons soy sauce
3 pounds pork shoulder
Salt and pepper to taste
Directions:
1.   Place all Ingredients in bowl and allow the meat to marinate in the fridge for at least 2 hours.
2.   Preheat the air fryer to 390°F.
3.   Place the grill pan accessory in the air fryer.
4.   Grill the meat for 20 minutes making sure to flip the pork every 10 minutes for even grilling and cook in batches.
5.   Meanwhile, pour the marinade in a saucepan and allow to simmer for 10 minutes until the sauce thickens.
6.   Baste the pork with the sauce before serving.
PER SERVING: CALORIES: 688; FAT: 52G; PROTEIN:17G

Chinese Salt and Pepper Pork Chop Stir-fry

Prep: 10 Minutes • Cook Time: 15 Minutes • Total: 25 Minutes
Serves: 4
Ingredients
Pork Chops:
Olive oil
¾ C. almond flour
¼ tsp. pepper
½ tsp. salt
1 egg white
Pork Chops
Stir-fry:
¼ tsp. pepper
1 tsp. sea salt
2 tbsp. olive oil
2 sliced scallions
2 sliced jalapeno peppers
Directions:
1.   Coat the air fryer oven basket with olive oil.
2.   Whisk pepper, salt, and egg white together till foamy.
3.   Cut pork chops into pieces, leaving just a bit on bones. Pat dry.
4.   Add pieces of pork to egg white mixture, coating well. Let sit for marinade 20 minutes.
5.   Put marinated chops into a large bowl and add almond flour. Dredge and shake off excess and place into air fryer.
6.   Set temperature to 360°F, and set time to 12 minutes. Cook 12 minutes at 360 degrees.
7.   Turn up the heat to 400 degrees and cook another 6 minutes till pork chops are nice and crisp.
8.   To make stir-fry, remove jalapeno seeds and chop up. Chop scallions and mix with jalapeno pieces.
9.   Heat a skillet with olive oil. Stir-fry pepper, salt, scallions, and jalapenos 60 seconds. Then add fried pork pieces to skills and toss with scallion mixture. Stir-fry 1-2 minutes till well coated and hot.
PER SERVING: CALORIES: 294; FAT: 17G; PROTEIN:36G; SUGAR:4G

Roasted Pork Tenderloin

Prep: 5 Minutes • Cook Time: 1 Hour • Total: 65 Minutes
Serves: 4
Ingredients
1 (3-pound) pork tenderloin
2 tablespoons extra-virgin olive oil
2 garlic cloves, minced
1 teaspoon dried basil
1 teaspoon dried oregano
1 teaspoon dried thyme
Salt
Pepper
Directions:
1.   Drizzle the pork tenderloin with the olive oil.
2.   Rub the garlic, basil, oregano, thyme, and salt and pepper to taste all over the tenderloin.
3.   Pour into the Oven rack/basket. Place the Rack on the middle-shelf of the Air fryer oven. Set temperature to 350°F, and set time to 45 minutes. Use a meat thermometer to test for doneness
4.   Open the air fryer and flip the pork tenderloin. Cook for an additional 15 minutes.
5.   Remove the cooked pork from the air fryer and allow it to rest for 10 minutes before cutting.
PER SERVING: CALORIES: 283; FAT: 10G; PROTEIN:48G

Garlic Putter Pork Chops

Prep: 10 Minutes • Cook Time: 7 Minutes • Total: 17 Minutes
Serves: 4
Ingredients
2 tsp. parsley
2 tsp. grated garlic cloves
1 tbsp. coconut oil
1 tbsp. coconut butter
4 pork chops
Directions:
1.   Ensure your air fryer oven is preheated to 350 degrees.
2.   Mix butter, coconut oil, and all seasoning together. Then rub seasoning mixture over all sides of pork chops. Place in foil, seal, and chill for 1 hour.
3.   Remove pork chops from foil and place into air fryer.
4.   Pour into the Oven rack/basket. Place the Rack on the middle-shelf of the Air fryer oven. Set temperature to 350°F, and set time to 7 minutes. Cook 7 minutes on one side and 8 minutes on the other.
5.   Drizzle with olive oil and serve alongside a green salad.
PER SERVING: CALORIES: 526; FAT: 23G; PROTEIN:41G; SUGAR:4G

Fried Pork with Sweet and Sour Glaze

Prep: 5 Minutes • Cook Time: 30 Minutes • Total: 35 Minutes
Serves: 4
Ingredients
¼ cup rice wine vinegar
¼ teaspoon Chinese five spice powder
1 cup potato starch
1 green onion, chopped
2 large eggs, beaten
2 pounds pork chops cut into chunks
2 tablespoons cornstarch + 3 tablespoons water
5 tablespoons brown sugar
Salt and pepper to taste
Directions:
1. Preheat the air fryer oven to 390°F.
2. Season pork chops with salt and pepper to taste.
3. Dip the pork chops in egg. Set aside.
4. In a bowl, combine the potato starch and Chinese five spice powder.
5. Dredge the pork chops in the flour mixture.
6. Place in the double layer rack and cook for 30 minutes.
7. Meanwhile, place the vinegar and brown sugar in a saucepan. Season with salt and pepper to taste. Stir in the cornstarch slurry and allow to simmer until thick.
8. Serve the pork chops with the sauce and garnish with green onions.
PER SERVING: CALORIES: 420; FAT: 11.8G; PROTEIN:69.2G

Oregano-Paprika on Breaded Pork

Prep: 10 Minutes • Cook Time: 30 Minutes • Total: 40 Minutes
Serves: 4
Ingredients
¼ cup water
¼ teaspoon dry mustard
½ teaspoon black pepper
½ teaspoon cayenne pepper
½ teaspoon garlic powder
½ teaspoon salt
1 cup panko breadcrumbs
1 egg, beaten
2 teaspoons oregano
4 lean pork chops
4 teaspoons paprika
Directions:
1. Preheat the air fryer oven to 390°F.
2. Pat dry the pork chops.
3. In a mixing bowl, combine the egg and water. Then set aside.
4. In another bowl, combine the rest of the Ingredients.
5. Dip the pork chops in the egg mixture and dredge in the flour mixture.
6. Place in the air fryer basket and cook for 25 to 30 minutes until golden.
PER SERVING: CALORIES: 364; FAT: 20.2G; PROTEIN:42.9G

Bacon Wrapped Pork Tenderloin

Prep: 5 Minutes • Cook Time: 15 Minutes • Total: 20 Minutes
Serves: 4

Ingredients

Pork:

1-2 tbsp. Dijon mustard
3-4 strips of bacon
1 pork tenderloin

Apple Gravy:

½ - 1 tsp. Dijon mustard
1 tbsp. almond flour
2 tbsp. ghee
1 chopped onion
2-3 Granny Smith apples
1 C. vegetable broth

Directions:

1. Spread Dijon mustard all over tenderloin and wrap meat with strips of bacon.
2. Pour into the Oven rack/basket. Place the Rack on the middle-shelf of the Air fryer oven. Set temperature to 360°F, and set time to 15 minutes. Use a meat thermometer to check for doneness.
3. To make sauce, heat ghee in a pan and add shallots. Cook 1-2 minutes.
4. Then add apples, cooking 3-5 minutes until softened.
5. Add flour and ghee to make a roux. Add broth and mustard, stirring well to combine.
6. When sauce starts to bubble, add 1 cup of sautéed apples, cooking till sauce thickens.
7. Once pork tenderloin I cook, allow to sit 5-10 minutes to rest before slicing.
8. Serve topped with apple gravy. Devour!

PER SERVING: CALORIES: 552; FAT: 25G; PROTEIN:29G; SUGAR:6G

Dijon Garlic Pork Tenderloin

Prep: 5 Minutes • Cook Time: 10 Minutes • Total: 15 Minutes
Serves: 6

Ingredients

1 C. breadcrumbs
Pinch of cayenne pepper
3 crushed garlic cloves
2 tbsp. ground ginger
2 tbsp. Dijon mustard
2 tbsp. raw honey
4 tbsp. water
2 tsp. salt
1 pound pork tenderloin, sliced into 1-inch rounds

Directions:

1. With pepper and salt, season all sides of tenderloin.
2. Combine cayenne pepper, garlic, ginger, mustard, honey, and water until smooth.
3. Dip pork rounds into honey mixture and then into breadcrumbs, ensuring they all get coated well.
4. Place coated pork rounds into your air fryer oven.
5. Pour into the Oven rack/basket. Place the Rack on the middle-shelf of the Air fryer oven. Set temperature to 400°F, and set time to 10 minutes. Cook 10 minutes at 400 degrees. Flip and then cook an additional 5 minutes until golden in color.

PER SERVING: CALORIES: 423; FAT: 18G; PROTEIN:31G; SUGAR:3G

Pork Neck with Salad

Prep: 10 Minutes • Cook Time: 12 Minutes • Total: 22 Minutes
Serves: 2
Ingredients
For Pork:
1 tablespoon soy sauce
1 tablespoon fish sauce
½ tablespoon oyster sauce
½ pound pork neck
For Salad:
1 ripe tomato, sliced tickly
8-10 Thai shallots, sliced
1 scallion, chopped
1 bunch fresh basil leaves
1 bunch fresh cilantro leaves
For Dressing:
3 tablespoons fish sauce
2 tablespoons olive oil
1 teaspoon apple cider vinegar
1 tablespoon palm sugar
2 bird eye chili
1 tablespoon garlic, minced
Directions:
1.   For pork in a bowl, mix together all ingredients except pork.
2.   Add pork neck and coat with marinade evenly. Refrigerate for about 2-3 hours.
3.   Preheat the air fryer oven to 340 degrees F.
4.   Place the pork neck onto a grill pan. Cook for about 12 minutes.
5.   Meanwhile in a large salad bowl, mix together all salad ingredients.
6.   In a bowl, add all dressing ingredients and beat till well combined.
7.   Remove pork neck from Air fryer and cut into desired slices.
8.   Place pork slices over salad.

Cajun Pork Steaks

Prep: 5 Minutes • Cook Time: 20 Minutes • Total: 25 Minutes
Serves: 6
Ingredients
4-6 pork steaks
BBQ sauce:
Cajun seasoning
1 tbsp. vinegar
1 tsp. low-sodium soy sauce
½ C. brown sugar
½ C. vegan ketchup
Directions:
1.   Ensure your air fryer oven is preheated to 290 degrees.
2.   Sprinkle pork steaks with Cajun seasoning.
3.   Combine remaining ingredients and brush onto steaks. Add coated steaks to air fryer.
4.   Pour into the Oven rack/basket. Place the Rack on the middle-shelf of the Air fryer oven. Set temperature to 290°F, and set time to 20 minutes. Cook 15-20 minutes till just browned.
PER SERVING: CALORIES: 209; FAT: 11G; PROTEIN:28G; SUGAR:2G

Wonton Taco Cups

Prep: 5 Minutes • Cook Time: 10 Minutes • Total: 15 Minutes
Serves: 8
Ingredients
1/2 pound ground pork, browned and drained
1/2 pound ground beef, browned and drained
1 envelope taco seasoning
1 (10-ounce) can tomatoes with chilies, diced and drained
1 bell pepper, seeded and chopped
32 wonton wrappers
1 cup Cheddar cheese, shredded
Directions:
1.   Combine the pork, beef, taco seasoning, diced tomatoes, and bell pepper; mix well.
2.   Line all the muffin cups with wonton wrappers. Spritz with a nonstick cooking oil. Divide the beef filling among wrappers; top with the shredded cheese.
3.   Pour into the Oven rack/basket. Place the Rack on the middle-shelf of the Air fryer oven. Set temperature to 370°F, and set time to 10 minutes. Bake at 370 degrees F for about 10 minutes or until heated through.

Cajun Sweet-Sour Grilled Pork

Prep: 5 Minutes • Cook Time: 12 Minutes • Total: 17 Minutes
Serves: 3
Ingredients
¼ cup brown sugar
1/4 cup cider vinegar
1-lb pork loin, sliced into 1-inch cubes
2 tablespoons Cajun seasoning
3 tablespoons brown sugar
Directions:
1.   In a shallow dish, mix well pork loin, 3 tablespoons brown sugar, and Cajun seasoning. Toss well to coat. Marinate in the ref for 3 hours.
2.   In a medium bowl mix well, brown sugar and vinegar for basting.
3.   Thread pork pieces in skewers. Baste with sauce and place on skewer rack in air fryer.
4.   For 12 minutes, cook on 360°F. Halfway through cooking time, turnover skewers and baste with sauce. If needed, cook in batches.
5.   Serve and enjoy.
PER SERVING: CALORIES: 428; FAT: 16.7G; PROTEIN:39G; SUGAR:2G

Chinese Braised Pork Belly

Prep: 5 Minutes • Cook Time: 20 Minutes • Total: 25 Minutes
Serves: 8
Ingredients
1 lb Pork Belly, sliced
1 Tbsp Oyster Sauce
1 Tbsp Sugar
2 Red Fermented Bean Curds
1 Tbsp Red Fermented Bean Curd Paste
1 Tbsp Cooking Wine
1/2 Tbsp Soy Sauce
1 Tsp Sesame Oil
1 Cup All Purpose Flour
Directions:
1.   Preheat the air fryer oven to 390 degrees.
2.   In a small bowl, mix all ingredients together and rub the pork thoroughly with this mixture
3.   Set aside to marinate for at least 30 minutes or preferably overnight for the flavors to permeate the meat
4.   Coat each marinated pork belly slice in flour and place in the air fryer tray
5.   Cook for 15 to 20 minutes until crispy and tender.

Air Fryer Sweet and Sour Pork

Prep: 10 Minutes • Cook Time: 12 Minutes • Total: 22 Minutes
Serves: 6
Ingredients
3 tbsp. olive oil
1/16 tsp. Chinese Five Spice
¼ tsp. pepper
½ tsp. sea salt
1 tsp. pure sesame oil
2 eggs
1 C. almond flour
2 pounds pork, sliced into chunks
 Sweet and Sour Sauce:
¼ tsp. sea salt
½ tsp. garlic powder
1 tbsp. low-sodium soy sauce
½ C. rice vinegar
5 tbsp. tomato paste
1/8 tsp. water
½ C. sweetener of choice

Directions:
1.　　To make the dipping sauce, whisk all sauce ingredients together over medium heat, stirring 5 minutes. Simmer uncovered 5 minutes till thickened.
2.　　Meanwhile, combine almond flour, five spice, pepper, and salt.
3.　　In another bowl, mix eggs with sesame oil.
4.　　Dredge pork in flour mixture and then in egg mixture. Shake any excess off before adding to air fryer basket.
5.　　Pour into the Oven rack/basket. Place the Rack on the middle-shelf of the Air fryer oven. Set temperature to 340°F, and set time to 12 minutes. Serve with sweet and sour dipping sauce.
PER SERVING: CALORIES: 371; FAT: 17G; PROTEIN:27G; SUGAR:1G

Pork Loin with Potatoes

Prep: 10 Minutes • Cook Time: 25 Minutes • Total: 35 Minutes
Serves: 2
Ingredients
2 pounds pork loin
1 teaspoon fresh parsley, chopped
2 large red potatoes, chopped
½ teaspoon garlic powder
½ teaspoon red pepper flakes, crushed
Salt and freshly ground black pepper, to taste

Directions:
1.　　In a large bowl, add all ingredients except glaze and toss to coat well. Preheat the Air fryer oven to 325 degrees F. Place the loin in the air fryer basket.
2.　　Arrange the potatoes around pork loin.
3.　　Cook for about 25 minutes.

Roasted Char Siew (Pork Butt)

Prep: 10 Minutes • Cook Time: 25 Minutes • Total: 35 Minutes
Serves: 6
Ingredients
1 strip of pork shoulder butt with a good amount of fat marbling
Marinade:
1 tsp. sesame oil
4 tbsp. raw honey
1 tsp. low-sodium dark soy sauce
1 tsp. light soy sauce
1 tbsp. rose wine
2 tbsp. Hoisin sauce
Directions:
1. Combine all marinade ingredients together and add to Ziploc bag. Place pork in bag, making sure all sections of pork strip are engulfed in the marinade. Chill 3-24 hours.
2. Take out the strip 30 minutes before planning to cook and preheat your air fryer oven to 350 degrees.
3. Place foil on small pan and brush with olive oil. Place marinated pork strip onto prepared pan.
4. Set temperature to 350°F, and set time to 20 minutes. Roast 20 minutes.
5. Glaze with marinade every 5-10 minutes.
6. Remove strip and leave to cool a few minutes before slicing.
PER SERVING: CALORIES: 289; FAT: 13G; PROTEIN:33G; SUGAR:1G

Juicy Pork Ribs Ole

Prep: 10 Minutes • Cook Time: 25 Minutes • Total: 35 Minutes
Serves: 4
Ingredients
1 rack of pork ribs
1/2 cup low-fat milk
1 tablespoon envelope taco seasoning mix
1 can tomato sauce
1/2 teaspoon ground black pepper
1 teaspoon seasoned salt
1 tablespoon cornstarch
1 teaspoon canola oil
Directions:
1. Place all ingredients in a mixing dish; let them marinate for 1 hour.
2. Pour into the Oven rack/basket. Place the Rack on the middle-shelf of the Air fryer oven. Set temperature to 390°F, and set time to 25 minutes. Cook the marinated ribs approximately 25 minutes.
3. Work with batches. Enjoy

Teriyaki Pork Rolls

Prep: 10 Minutes • Cook Time: 8 Minutes • Total: 20 Minutes
Serves: 6
Ingredients
1 tsp. almond flour
4 tbsp. low-sodium soy sauce
4 tbsp. mirin
4 tbsp. brown sugar
Thumb-sized amount of ginger, chopped
Pork belly slices
Enoki mushrooms
Directions:
1. *Mix brown sugar, mirin, soy sauce, almond flour, and ginger together until brown sugar dissolves.*
2. *Take pork belly slices and wrap around a bundle of mushrooms. Brush each roll with teriyaki sauce. Chill half an hour.*
3. Preheat your air fryer oven to 350 degrees and add marinated pork rolls.
4. Pour into the Oven rack/basket. Place the Rack on the middle-shelf of the Air fryer oven. Set temperature to 350°F, and set time to 8 minutes.
PER SERVING: CALORIES: 412; FAT: 9G; PROTEIN:19G; SUGAR:4G

Ham and Cheese Rollups

Prep: 5 Minutes • Cook Time: 8 Minutes • Total: 15 Minutes
Serves: 12
Ingredients
2 tsp. raw honey
2 tsp. dried parsley
1 tbsp. poppy seeds
½ C. melted coconut oil
¼ C. spicy brown mustard
9 slices of provolone cheese
10 ounces of thinly sliced Black Forest Ham
1 tube of crescent rolls
Directions:
1.   Roll out dough into a rectangle. Spread 2-3 tablespoons of spicy mustard onto dough, then layer provolone cheese and ham slices.
2.   Roll the filled dough up as tight as you can and slice into 12-15 pieces.
3.   Melt coconut oil and mix with a pinch of salt and pepper, parsley, honey, and remaining mustard.
4.   Brush mustard mixture over roll-ups and sprinkle with poppy seeds.
5.   Grease air fryer basket liberally with olive oil and add rollups.
6.   Set temperature to 350°F, and set time to 8 minutes.
PER SERVING: CALORIES: 289; FAT: 6G; PROTEIN:18G; SUGAR

Vietnamese Pork Chops

Prep: 10 Minutes • Cook Time: 7 Minutes • Total: 25 Minutes
Serves: 6
Ingredients
1 tbsp. olive oil
1 tbsp. fish sauce
1 tsp. low-sodium dark soy sauce
1 tsp. pepper
3 tbsp. lemongrass
1 tbsp. chopped shallot
1 tbsp. chopped garlic
1 tbsp. brown sugar
2 pork chops
Directions:
1.   Add pork chops to a bowl along with olive oil, fish sauce, soy sauce, pepper, lemongrass, shallot, garlic, and brown sugar.
2.   Marinade pork chops 2 hours.
3.   Ensure your air fryer is preheated to 400 degrees. Add pork chops to the basket.
4.   Pour into the Oven rack/basket. Place the Rack on the middle-shelf of the Air fryer oven. Set temperature to 400°F, and set time to 7 minutes. Cook making sure to flip after 5 minutes of cooking.
5.   Serve alongside steamed cauliflower rice.
PER SERVING: CALORIES: 290; FAT: 15G; PROTEIN:30G; SUGAR:3G

Beef Recipes

Cheeseburger Egg Rolls

Prep: 10 Minutes • Cook Time: 7 Minutes • Total: 17 Minutes
Serves: 6
Ingredients
6 egg roll wrappers
6 chopped dill pickle chips
1 tbsp. yellow mustard
3 tbsp. cream cheese
3 tbsp. shredded cheddar cheese
½ C. chopped onion
½ C. chopped bell pepper
¼ tsp. onion powder
¼ tsp. garlic powder
8 ounces of raw lean ground beef
Directions:
1.   In a skillet, add seasonings, beef, onion, and bell pepper. Stir and crumble beef till fully cooked, and vegetables are soft.
2.   Take skillet off the heat and add cream cheese, mustard, and cheddar cheese, stirring till melted.
3.   Pour beef mixture into a bowl and fold in pickles.
4.   Lay out egg wrappers and place 1/6th of beef mixture into each one. Moisten egg roll wrapper edges with water. Fold sides to the middle and seal with water.
5.   Repeat with all other egg rolls.
6.   Place rolls into air fryer, one batch at a time.
7.   Pour into the Oven rack/basket. Place the Rack on the middle-shelf of the Air fryer oven. Set temperature to 392°F, and set time to 7 minutes.
PER SERVING: CALORIES: 153; FAT: 4G; PROTEIN:12G; SUGAR:3G

Air Fried Grilled Steak

Prep: 5 Minutes • Cook Time: 45 Minutes • Total: 50 Minutes
Serves: 2
Ingredients
2 top sirloin steaks
3 tablespoons butter, melted
3 tablespoons olive oil
Salt and pepper to taste
Directions:
1.   Preheat the air fryer oven for 5 minutes.
2.   Season the sirloin steaks with olive oil, salt and pepper.
3.   Place the beef in the air fryer basket.
4.   Cook for 45 minutes at 350°F.
5.   Once cooked, serve with butter.
PER SERVING: CALORIES: 1536; FAT: 123.7G; PROTEIN:103.4G

Juicy Cheeseburgers

Prep: 5 Minutes • Cook Time: 15 Minutes • Total: 20 Minutes
Serves: 4
Ingredients
1 pound 93% lean ground beef
1 teaspoon Worcestershire sauce
1 tablespoon burger seasoning
Salt
Pepper
Cooking oil
4 slices cheese
buns
Directions:
1.   In a large bowl, mix the ground beef, Worcestershire, burger seasoning, and salt and pepper to taste until well blended. Spray the air fryer basket with cooking oil. You will need only a quick spritz. The burgers will produce oil as they cook. Shape the mixture into 4 patties. Place the burgers in the air fryer. The burgers should fit without the need to stack, but stacking is okay if necessary.
2.   Pour into the Oven rack/basket. Place the Rack on the middle-shelf of the Air fryer oven. Set temperature to 375°F, and set time to 8 minutes.Cook for 8 minutes. Open and flip the burgers and cook for an additional 3 to 4 minutes. Check the inside of the burgers. You can stick a knife in the center to examine the color.
3.   Top each burger with a slice of cheese. Cook until the cheese has melted, about 1 minute. Serve on buns with any additional toppings of your choice.
PER SERVING: CALORIES: 566; FAT: 39G; PROTEIN:29G; FIBER:1G

Spicy Thai Beef Stir-Fry

Prep: 15 Minutes • Cook Time: 9 Minutes • Total: 24 Minutes
Serves: 4
Ingredients
1 pound sirloin steaks, thinly sliced
2 tablespoons lime juice, divided
⅓ cup crunchy peanut butter
½ cup beef broth
1 tablespoon olive oil
1½ cups broccoli florets
2 cloves garlic, sliced
1 to 2 red chile peppers, sliced
Directions:
1.   In a medium bowl, combine the steak with 1 tablespoon of the lime juice. Set aside.
2.   Combine the peanut butter and beef broth in a small bowl and mix well. Drain the beef and add the juice from the bowl into the peanut butter mixture.
3.   In a 6-inch metal bowl, combine the olive oil, steak, and broccoli.
4.   Pour into the Oven rack/basket. Place the Rack on the middle-shelf of the Air fryer oven. Set temperature to 375°F, and set time to 4 minutes. Cook for 3 to 4 minutes or until the steak is almost cooked and the broccoli is crisp and tender, shaking the basket once during cooking time.
5.   Add the garlic, chile peppers, and the peanut butter mixture and stir.
6.   Cook for 3 to 5 minutes or until the sauce is bubbling and the broccoli is tender.
7.   Serve over hot rice.
PER SERVING: CALORIES: 387; FAT: 22G; PROTEIN:42G; FIBER:2G

Beef Brisket Recipe from Texas

Prep: 15 Minutes • Cook Time: 1Hour And 30 Minutes Minutes
Serves: 8
Ingredients
1 ½ cup beef stock
1 bay leaf
1 tablespoon garlic powder
1 tablespoon onion powder
2 pounds beef brisket, trimmed
2 tablespoons chili powder
2 teaspoons dry mustard
4 tablespoons olive oil
Salt and pepper to taste
Directions:
1. Preheat the air fryer oven for 5 minutes. Place all ingredients in a deep baking dish that will fit in the air fryer.
2. Bake for 1 hour and 30 minutes at 400°F.
3. Stir the beef every after 30 minutes to soak in the sauce.
PER SERVING: CALORIES: 306; FAT: 24.1G; PROTEIN:18.3G

Copycat Taco Bell Crunch Wraps

Prep: 10 Minutes • Cook Time: 2 Minutes • Total: 15 Minutes
Serves: 6
Ingredients
6 wheat tostadas
2 C. sour cream
2 C. Mexican blend cheese
2 C. shredded lettuce
12 ounces low-sodium nacho cheese
3 Roma tomatoes
6 12-inch wheat tortillas
1 1/3 C. water
2 packets low-sodium taco seasoning
2 pounds of lean ground beef
Directions:
1. Ensure your air fryer is preheated to 400 degrees.
2. Make beef according to taco seasoning packets.
3. Place 2/3 C. prepared beef, 4 tbsp. cheese, 1 tostada, 1/3 C. sour cream, 1/3 C. lettuce, 1/6th of tomatoes and 1/3 C. cheese on each tortilla.
4. Fold up tortillas edges and repeat with remaining ingredients.
5. Lay the folded sides of tortillas down into the air fryer and spray with olive oil.
6. Set temperature to 400°F, and set time to 2 minutes. Cook 2 minutes till browned.
PER SERVING: CALORIES: 311; FAT: 9G; PROTEIN:22G; SUGAR:2G

Air Fryer Beef Casserole

Prep: 5 Minutes • Cook Time: 30 Minutes • Total: 35 Minutes
Serves: 4
Ingredients
1 green bell pepper, seeded and chopped
1 onion, chopped
1-pound ground beef
3 cloves of garlic, minced
3 tablespoons olive oil
6 cups eggs, beaten
Salt and pepper to taste
Directions:
1.   Preheat the air fryer oven for 5 minutes.
2.   In a baking dish that will fit in the air fryer, mix the ground beef, onion, garlic, olive oil, and bell pepper. Season with salt and pepper to taste.
3.   Pour in the beaten eggs and give a good stir.
4.   Place the dish with the beef and egg mixture in the air fryer.
5.   Pour into the Oven rack/basket. Place the Rack on the middle-shelf of the Air fryer oven. Set temperature to 325°F, and set time to 30 minutes. Bake for 30 minutes.
PER SERVING: CALORIES: 1520; FAT: 125.11G; PROTEIN:87.9G

Meat Lovers' Pizza

Prep: 10 Minutes • Cook Time: 12 Minutes • Total: 22 Minutes
Serves: 2
Ingredients
1 pre-prepared 7-inch pizza pie crust, defrosted if necessary.
1/3 cup of marinara sauce.
2 ounces of grilled steak, sliced into bite-sized pieces
2 ounces of salami, sliced fine
2 ounces of pepperoni, sliced fine
¼ cup of American cheese
¼ cup of shredded mozzarella cheese
Directions:
1.   Preheat the air fryer oven to 350 degrees. Lay the pizza dough flat on a sheet of parchment paper or tin foil, cut large enough to hold the entire pie crust, but small enough that it will leave the edges of the air frying basket uncovered to allow for air circulation. Using a fork, stab the pizza dough several times across the surface – piercing the pie crust will allow air to circulate throughout the crust and ensure even cooking. With a deep soup spoon, ladle the marinara sauce onto the pizza dough, and spread evenly in expanding circles over the surface of the pie-crust. Be sure to leave at least ½ inch of bare dough around the edges, to ensure that extra-crispy crunchy first bite of the crust! Distribute the pieces of steak and the slices of salami and pepperoni evenly over the sauce-covered dough, then sprinkle the cheese in an even layer on top.
2.   Set the air fryer timer to 12 minutes, and place the pizza with foil or paper on the fryer's basket surface. Again, be sure to leave the edges of the basket uncovered to allow for proper air circulation, and don't let your bare fingers touch the hot surface. After 12 minutes, when the air fryer oven shuts off, the cheese should be perfectly melted and lightly crisped, and the pie crust should be golden brown. Using a spatula – or two, if necessary, remove the pizza from the air fryer basket and set on a serving plate. Wait a few minutes until the pie is cool enough to handle, then cut into slices and serve.

Chimichurri Skirt Steak

Prep: 10 Minutes • Cook Time: 8 Minutes • Total: 18 Minutes
Serves: 2
Ingredients
2 x 8 oz Skirt Steak
1 cup Finely Chopped Parsley
¼ cup Finely Chopped Mint
2 Tbsp Fresh Oregano (Washed & finely chopped)
3 Finely Chopped Cloves of Garlic
1 Tsp Red Pepper Flakes (Crushed)
1 Tbsp Ground Cumin
1 Tsp Cayenne Pepper
2 Tsp Smoked Paprika
1 Tsp Salt
¼ Tsp Pepper
¾ cup Oil
3 Tbsp Red Wine Vinegar
Directions:
1.   Throw all the ingredients in a bowl (besides the steak) and mix well.
2.   Put ¼ cup of the mixture in a plastic baggie with the steak and leave in the fridge overnight (2–24hrs).
3.   Leave the bag out at room temperature for at least 30 min before popping into the air fryer. Preheat for a minute or two to 390° F before cooking until med–rare (8–10 min). Pour into the Oven rack/basket. Place the Rack on the middle-shelf of the Air fryer oven. Set temperature to 390°F, and set time to 10 minutes.
4.   Put 2 Tbsp of the chimichurri mix on top of each steak before serving.

Country Fried Steak

Prep: 5 Minutes • Cook Time: 12 Minutes • Total: 20 Minutes
Serves: 2
Ingredients
1 tsp. pepper
2 C. almond milk
2 tbsp. almond flour
6 ounces ground sausage meat
1 tsp. pepper
1 tsp. salt
1 tsp. garlic powder
1 tsp. onion powder
1 C. panko breadcrumbs
1 C. almond flour
3 beaten eggs
6 ounces sirloin steak, pounded till thin
Directions:
1.   Season panko breadcrumbs with spices.
2.   Dredge steak in flour, then egg, and then seasoned panko mixture.
3.   Place into air fryer basket.
4.   Set temperature to 370°F, and set time to 12 minutes.
5.   To make sausage gravy, cook sausage and drain off fat, but reserve 2 tablespoons.
6.   Add flour to sausage and mix until incorporated. Gradually mix in milk over medium to high heat till it becomes thick.
7.   Season mixture with pepper and cook 3 minutes longer.
8.   Serve steak topped with gravy and enjoy.
PER SERVING: CALORIES: 395; FAT: 11G; PROTEIN:39G; SUGAR:5G

Creamy Burger & Potato Bake

Prep: 5 Minutes • Cook Time: 55 Minutes • Total: 60 Minutes
Serves: 3
Ingredients
salt to taste
freshly ground pepper, to taste
1/2 (10.75 ounce) can condensed cream of mushroom soup
1/2-pound lean ground beef
1-1/2 cups peeled and thinly sliced potatoes
1/2 cup shredded Cheddar cheese
1/4 cup chopped onion
1/4 cup and 2 tablespoons milk
Directions:
1.   Lightly grease baking pan of air fryer with cooking spray. Add ground beef. For 10 minutes, cook on 360°F. Stir and crumble halfway through cooking time.
2.   Meanwhile, in a bowl, whisk well pepper, salt, milk, onion, and mushroom soup. Mix well.
3.   Drain fat off ground beef and transfer beef to a plate.
4.   In same air fryer baking pan, layer ½ of potatoes on bottom, then ½ of soup mixture, and then ½ of beef. Repeat process.
5.   Cover pan with foil.
6.   Cook for 30 minutes. Remove foil and cook for another 15 minutes or until potatoes are tender.
7.   Serve and enjoy.
PER SERVING: CALORIES: 399; FAT: 26.9G; PROTEIN:22.1G

Beefy 'n Cheesy Spanish Rice Casserole

Prep: 10 Minutes • Cook Time: 50 Minutes • Total: 60 Minutes
Serves: 3
Ingredients
2 tablespoons chopped green bell pepper
1 tablespoon chopped fresh cilantro
1/2-pound lean ground beef
1/2 cup water
1/2 teaspoon salt
1/2 teaspoon brown sugar
1/2 pinch ground black pepper
1/3 cup uncooked long grain rice
1/4 cup finely chopped onion
1/4 cup chile sauce
1/4 teaspoon ground cumin
1/4 teaspoon Worcestershire sauce
1/4 cup shredded Cheddar cheese
1/2 (14.5 ounce) can canned tomatoes
Directions:
1.   Lightly grease baking pan of air fryer with cooking spray. Add ground beef.
2.   For 10 minutes, cook on 360°F. Halfway through cooking time, stir and crumble beef. Discard excess fat,
3.   Stir in pepper, Worcestershire sauce, cumin, brown sugar, salt, chile sauce, rice, water, tomatoes, green bell pepper, and onion. Mix well. Cover pan with foil and cook for 25 minutes. Stirring occasionally.
4.   Give it one last good stir, press down firmly and sprinkle cheese on top.
5.   Cook uncovered for 15 minutes at 390°F until tops are lightly browned.
6.   Serve and enjoy with chopped cilantro.
PER SERVING: CALORIES: 346; FAT: 19.1G; PROTEIN:18.5G

Warming Winter Beef with Celery

Prep: 5 Minutes • Cook Time: 12 Minutes • Total: 15 Minutes
Serves: 4
Ingredients
9 ounces tender beef, chopped
1/2 cup leeks, chopped
1/2 cup celery stalks, chopped
2 cloves garlic, smashed
2 tablespoons red cooking wine
3/4 cup cream of celery soup
2 sprigs rosemary, chopped
1/4 teaspoon smoked paprika
3/4 teaspoons salt
1/4 teaspoon black pepper, or to taste
Directions:
1.   Add the beef, leeks, celery, and garlic to the baking dish; cook for about 5 minutes at 390 degrees F.
2.   Once the meat is starting to tender, pour in the wine and soup. Season with rosemary, smoked paprika, salt, and black pepper. Now, cook an additional 7 minutes.

Beef & veggie Spring Rolls

PREP: 5 MINUTES • COOK TIME: 12 MINUTES • TOTAL: 55 MINUTES
SERVES: 10
Ingredients
2-ounce Asian rice noodles
1 tablespoon sesame oil
7-ounce ground beef
1 small onion, chopped
3 garlic cloves, crushed
1 cup fresh mixed vegetables
1 teaspoon soy sauce
1 packet spring roll skins
2 tablespoons water
Olive oil, as required
Directions:
1.   Soak the noodles in warm water till soft.
2.   Drain and cut into small lengths. In a pan heat the oil and add the onion and garlic and sauté for about 4-5 minutes.
3.   Add beef and cook for about 4-5 minutes.
4.   Add vegetables and cook for about 5-7 minutes or till cooked through.
5.   Stir in soy sauce and remove from the heat.
6.   Immediately, stir in the noodles and keep aside till all the juices have been absorbed.
7.   Preheat the air fryer oven to 350 degrees F.
8.   Place the spring rolls skin onto a smooth surface.
9.   Add a line of the filling diagonally across.
10.   Fold the top point over the filling and then fold in both sides.
11.   On the final point brush it with water before rolling to seal.
12.   Brush the spring rolls with oil.
13.   Arrange the rolls in batches in the air fryer and Cook for about 8 minutes.
14.   Repeat with remaining rolls. Now, place spring rolls onto a baking sheet.
15.   Bake for about 6 minutes per side.

Charred Onions And Steak Cube BBQ

Prep: 5 Minutes • Cook Time: 40 Minutes • Total: 45 Minutes
Serves: 3
Ingredients
1 cup red onions, cut into wedges
1 tablespoon dry mustard
1 tablespoon olive oil
1-pound boneless beef sirloin, cut into cubes
Salt and pepper to taste
Directions:
1.   Preheat the air fryer to 390°F.
2.   Place the grill pan accessory in the air fryer.
3.   Toss all ingredients in a bowl and mix until everything is coated with the seasonings.
4.   Place on the grill pan and cook for 40 minutes.
5.   Halfway through the cooking time, give a stir to cook evenly.
PER SERVING: CALORIES: 260; FAT: 10.7G; PROTEIN:35.5G

Beef Stroganoff

Prep: 10 Minutes • Cook Time: 14 Minutes • Total: 24 Minutes
Serves: 4
Ingredients
9 Ozs Tender Beef
1 Onion, chopped
1 Tbsp Paprika
3/4 Cup Sour Cream
Salt and Pepper to taste
Baking Dish
Directions:
1.   Preheat the air fryer oven to 390 degrees.
2.   Chop the beef and marinate it with the paprika.
3.   Add the chopped onions into the baking dish and heat for about 2 minutes in the air fryer oven.
4.   When the onions are transparent, add the beef into the dish and cook for 5 minutes.
5.   Once the beef is starting to tender, pour in the sour cream and cook for another 7 minutes.
6.   At this point, the liquid should have reduced. Season with salt and pepper and serve.

Cheesy Ground Beef And Mac Taco Casserole

Prep: 10 Minutes • Cook Time: 25 Minutes • Total: 35 Minutes
Serves: 5
Ingredients
1-ounce shredded Cheddar cheese
1-ounce shredded Monterey Jack cheese
2 tablespoons chopped green onions
1/2 (10.75 ounce) can condensed tomato soup
1/2-pound lean ground beef
1/2 cup crushed tortilla chips
1/4-pound macaroni, cooked according to manufacturer's Instructions
1/4 cup chopped onion
1/4 cup sour cream (optional)
1/2 (1.25 ounce) package taco seasoning mix
1/2 (14.5 ounce) can diced tomatoes
Directions:
1.   Lightly grease baking pan of air fryer with cooking spray. Add onion and ground beef. For 10 minutes, cook on 360°F. Halfway through cooking time, stir and crumble ground beef.
2.   Add taco seasoning, diced tomatoes, and tomato soup. Mix well. Mix in pasta.
3.   Sprinkle crushed tortilla chips. Sprinkle cheese.
4.   Cook for 15 minutes at 390°F until tops are lightly browned and cheese is melted.
5.   Serve and enjoy.
PER SERVING: CALORIES: 329; FAT: 17G; PROTEIN:15.6G

Beefy Steak Topped with Chimichurri Sauce

Prep: 5 Minutes • Cook Time: 60 Minutes • Total: 65 Minutes
Serves: 6
Ingredients
1 cup commercial chimichurri
3 pounds steak
Salt and pepper to taste
Directions:
1. Place all ingredients in a Ziploc bag and marinate in the fridge for 2 hours.
2. Preheat the air fryer to 390°F.
3. Place the grill pan accessory in the air fryer.
4. Grill the skirt steak for 20 minutes per batch.
5. Flip the steak every 10 minutes for even grilling.
PER SERVING: CALORIES: 507; FAT: 27G; PROTEIN:63 G

Beef Ribeye Steak

Prep: 5 Minutes • Cook Time: 20 Minutes • Total: 25 Minutes
Serves: 4
Ingredients
4 (8-ounce) ribeye steaks
1 tablespoon McCormick Grill Mates Montreal Steak Seasoning
Salt
Pepper
Directions:
1. Season the steaks with the steak seasoning and salt and pepper to taste. Place 2 steaks in the air fryer oven. You can use an accessory grill pan, a layer rack, or the air fryer basket.
2. Set temperature to 390°F. Cook for 4 minutes. Open the air fryer and flip the steaks.
3. Cook for an additional 4 to 5 minutes. Check for doneness to determine how much additional cook time is need. Remove the cooked steaks from the air fryer oven, then repeat for the remaining 2 steaks. Cool before serving.
PER SERVING: CALORIES: 293; FAT: 22G; PROTEIN:23G; FIBER:0G

Air Fryer Roast Beef

Prep: 5 Minutes • Cook Time: 45 Minutes • Total: 50 Minutes
Serves: 6
Ingredients
Roast beef
1 tbsp. olive oil
Seasonings of choice
Directions:
1. Ensure your air fryer oven is preheated to 160 degrees.
2. Place roast in bowl and toss with olive oil and desired seasonings.
3. Put seasoned roast into air fryer.
4. Set temperature to 160°F, and set time to 30 minutes and cook 30 minutes.
5. Turn roast when the timer sounds and cook another 15 minutes.
PER SERVING: CALORIES: 267; FAT: 8G; PROTEIN:21G; SUGAR:1G

Beef Korma

Prep: 10 Minutes • Cook Time: 20 Minutes • Total: 30 Minutes
Serves: 6
Ingredients
½ cup yogurt
1 tablespoon curry powder
1 tablespoon olive oil
1 onion, chopped
2 cloves garlic, minced
1 tomato, diced
½ cup frozen baby peas, thawed
Directions:
1.   In a medium bowl, combine the steak, yogurt, and curry powder. Stir and set aside.
2.   In a 6-inch metal bowl, combine the olive oil, onion, and garlic.
3.   Set temperature to 390°F and cook for 3 to 4 minutes or until crisp and tender.
4.   Add the steak along with the yogurt and the diced tomato. Cook for 12 to 13 minutes or until steak is almost tender.
5.   Stir in the peas and cook for 2 to 3 minutes or until hot.
PER SERVING: CALORIES: 289; FAT: 11G; PROTEIN:38G; FIBER:2G

Cumin-Paprika Rubbed Beef Brisket

Prep: 5 Minutes • Cook Time: 2 Hours • Total: 2 Hours, 5 Minutes
Serves: 12
Ingredients
¼ teaspoon cayenne pepper
1 ½ tablespoons paprika
1 teaspoon garlic powder
1 teaspoon ground cumin
1 teaspoon onion powder
2 teaspoons dry mustard
2 teaspoons ground black pepper
2 teaspoons salt
5 pounds brisket roast
5 tablespoons olive oil
Directions:
1.   Place all ingredients in a Ziploc bag and allow to marinate in the fridge for at least 2 hours.
2.   Preheat the air fryer oven for 5 minutes.
3.   Place the meat in a baking dish that will fit in the air fryer.
4.   Place in the air fryer and cook for 2 hours at 350°F.
PER SERVING: CALORIES: 269; FAT: 12.8G; PROTEIN:35.6G; FIBER:2G

Chili-Espresso Marinated Steak

Prep: 5 Minutes • Cook Time: 50 Minutes• Total: 55 Minutes
Serves: 3
Ingredients
½ teaspoon garlic powder
1 ½ pounds beef flank steak
1 teaspoon instant espresso powder
2 tablespoons olive oil
2 teaspoons chili powder
Salt and pepper to taste
Directions:
1.	Preheat the air fryer oven to 390°F.
2.	Place the grill pan accessory in the air fryer.
3.	Make the dry rub by mixing the chili powder, salt, pepper, espresso powder, and garlic powder.
4.	Rub all over the steak and brush with oil.
5.	Place on the grill pan and cook for 40 minutes.
6.	Halfway through the cooking time, flip the beef to cook evenly.
PER SERVING: CALORIES: 249; FAT: 17G; PROTEIN:20G; FIBER:2G

Crispy Mongolian Beef

Prep: 5 Minutes • Cook Time: 10 Minutes • Total: 15 Minutes
Serves: 6
Ingredients
Olive oil
½ C. almond flour
2 pounds beef tenderloin or beef chuck, sliced into strips
Sauce:
½ C. chopped green onion
1 tsp. red chili flakes
1 tsp. almond flour
½ C. brown sugar
1 tsp. hoisin sauce
½ C. water
½ C. rice vinegar
½ C. low-sodium soy sauce
1 tbsp. chopped garlic
1 tbsp. finely chopped ginger
2 tbsp. olive oil
Directions:
1.	Toss strips of beef in almond flour, ensuring they are coated well. Add to the air fryer oven.
2.	Pour into the Oven rack/basket. Place the Rack on the middle-shelf of the Air fryer oven. Set temperature to 300°F, and set time to 10 minutes, and cook 10 minutes.
3.	Meanwhile, add all sauce ingredients to the pan and bring to a boil. Mix well.
4.	Add beef strips to the sauce and cook 2 minutes.
5.	Serve over cauliflower rice!
PER SERVING: CALORIES: 290; FAT: 14G; PROTEIN:22G; SUGAR:1G

Beef & Lemon Schnitzel for One

Prep: 5 Minutes • Cook Time: 12 Minutes • Total: 17 Minutes
Serves: 1
Ingredients
2 Tbsp Oil
2–3 oz Breadcrumbs
1 Whisked Egg in a Saucer/Soup Plate
1 Beef Schnitzel
1 Freshly Picked Lemon
Directions:
1.	Mix the oil and breadcrumbs together until loose and crumbly. Dip the meat into the egg, then into the crumbs. Make sure that it is evenly covered.
2.	Gently place in the air fryer basket, and cook at 350° F (preheat if needed) until done. The timing will depend on the thickness of the schnitzel, but for a relatively thin one, it should take roughly 12 min. Serve with a lemon half and a garden salad.

Crispy Beef Schnitzel

Prep: 5 Minutes • Cook Time: 12 Minutes • Total: 17 Minutes
Serves: 1
Ingredients
1 beef schnitzel
Salt and ground black pepper, to taste
2 tablespoons olive oil
1/3 cup breadcrumbs
1 egg, whisked
Directions:
1.	Season the schnitzel with salt and black pepper.
2.	In a mixing bowl, combine the oil and breadcrumbs. In another shallow bowl, beat the egg until frothy.
3.	Dip the schnitzel in the egg; then, dip it in the oil mixture.
4.	Pour into the Oven rack/basket. Place the Rack on the middle-shelf of the Air fryer oven. Set temperature to 350°F, and set time to 12 minutes.
5.	Enjoy!

Simple Steak

Prep: 6Minutes • Cook Time: 14 Minutes • Total: 20 Minutes
Serves: 2
Ingredients
½ pound quality cuts steak
Salt and freshly ground black pepper, to taste
Directions:
1.	Preheat the air fryer to 390 degrees F.
2.	Rub the steak with salt and pepper evenly.
3.	Place the steak in the air fryer basket and cook for about 14 minutes crispy.

Garlic-Cumin And Orange Juice Marinated Steak

Prep: 6 Minutes • Cook Time: 60 Minutes • Total: 66 Minutes
Serves: 4
Ingredients
¼ cup orange juice
1 teaspoon ground cumin
2 pounds skirt steak, trimmed from excess fat
2 tablespoons lime juice
2 tablespoons olive oil
4 cloves of garlic, minced
Salt and pepper to taste
Directions:
1.   Place all ingredients in a mixing bowl and allow to marinate in the fridge for at least 2 hours
2.   Preheat the air fryer oven to 390°F.
3.   Place the grill pan accessory in the air fryer.
4.   Grill for 15 minutes per batch and flip the beef every 8 minutes for even grilling.
5.   Meanwhile, pour the marinade on a saucepan and allow to simmer for 10 minutes or until the sauce thickens.
6.   Slice the beef and pour over the sauce.
PER SERVING: CALORIES: 568; FAT: 34.7G; PROTEIN:59.1G; SUGAR:1G

Beef Taco Fried Egg Rolls

Prep: 10 Minutes • Cook Time: 12 Minutes • Total: 25 Minutes
Serves: 8
Ingredients
1 tsp. cilantro
2 chopped garlic cloves
1 tbsp. olive oil
1 C. shredded Mexican cheese
½ packet taco seasoning
½ can cilantro lime rotel
½ chopped onion
16 egg roll wrappers
1 pound lean ground beef
Directions:
1.   Ensure that your air fryer oven is preheated to 400 degrees.
2.   Add onions and garlic to a skillet, cooking till fragrant. Then add taco seasoning, pepper, salt, and beef, cooking till beef is broke up into tiny pieces and cooked thoroughly.
3.   Add rotel and stir well.
4.   Lay out egg wrappers and brush with water to soften a bit.
5.   Load wrappers with beef filling and add cheese to each.
6.   Fold diagonally to close and use water to secure edges.
7.   Brush filled egg wrappers with olive oil and add to the air fryer.
8.   Pour into the Oven rack/basket. Place the Rack on the middle-shelf of the Air fryer oven. Set temperature to 400°F, and set time to 8 minutes. Cook 8 minutes, flip, and cook another 4 minutes.
9.   Served sprinkled with cilantro.
PER SERVING: CALORIES: 348; FAT: 11G; PROTEIN:24G; SUGAR:1G

Beef With Beans

Prep: 10 Minutes • Cook Time: 13 Minutes • Total: 23 Minutes
Serves: 8
Ingredients
12 Ozs Lean Steak
1 Onion, sliced
1 Can Chopped Tomatoes
3/4 Cup Beef Stock
4 Tsp Fresh Thyme, chopped
1 Can Red Kidney Beans
Salt and Pepper to taste
Oven Safe Bowl
Directions:
1.   Preheat the air fryer oven to 390 degrees.
2.   Trim the fat from the meat and cut into thin 1cm strips
3.   Add onion slices to the oven safe bowl and place in the air fryer.
4.   Pour into the Oven rack/basket. Place the Rack on the middle-shelf of the Air fryer oven. Set temperature to 390°F, and set time to 13 minutes, Cook for 3 minutes. Add the meat and continue cooking for 5 minutes.
5.   Add the tomatoes and their juice, beef stock, thyme and the beans and cook for an additional 5 minutes
6.   Season with black pepper to taste.

Swedish Meatballs

Prep: 10 Minutes • Cook Time: 14 Minutes • Total: 24 Minutes
Serves: 4
Ingredients
For the meatballs
1 pound 93% lean ground beef
1 (1-ounce) packet Lipton Onion Recipe Soup & Dip Mix
⅓ cup bread crumbs
1 egg, beaten
Salt
Pepper
For the gravy
1 cup beef broth
⅓ cup heavy cream
tablespoons all-purpose flour
Directions:
1.   In a large bowl, combine the ground beef, onion soup mix, bread crumbs, egg, and salt and pepper to taste. Mix thoroughly.
2.   Using 2 tablespoons of the meat mixture, create each meatball by rolling the beef mixture around in your hands. This should yield about 10 meatballs.
3.   Place the meatballs in the air fryer basket. It is okay to stack them. Set temperature to 390°Fand cook for 14 minutes.
4.   While the meatballs cook, prepare the gravy. Heat a saucepan over medium-high heat.
5.   Add the beef broth and heavy cream. Stir for 1 to 2 minutes.
6.   Add the flour and stir. Cover and allow the sauce to simmer for 3 to 4 minutes, or until thick.
7.   Drizzle the gravy over the meatballs and serve.
PER SERVING: CALORIES: 178; FAT: 14G; PROTEIN:9G; FIBER:0G

Rice and Meatball Stuffed Bell Peppers

Prep: 13 Minutes • Cook Time: 15 Minutes • Total: 28 Minutes

Serves: 4

Ingredients

4 bell peppers

1 tablespoon olive oil

1 small onion, chopped

2 cloves garlic, minced

1 cup frozen cooked rice, thawed

16 to 20 small frozen precooked meatballs, thawed

½ cup tomato sauce

tablespoons Dijon mustard

Directions:

1.   To prepare the peppers, cut off about ½ inch of the tops. Carefully remove the membranes and seeds from inside the peppers. Set aside.

2.   In a 6-by-6-by-2-inch pan, combine the olive oil, onion, and garlic.

3.   Set temperature to 360°F. Bake in the air fryer oven for 2 to 4 minutes or until crisp and tender. Remove the vegetable mixture from the pan and set aside in a medium bowl.

4.   Add the rice, meatballs, tomato sauce, and mustard to the vegetable mixture and stir to combine. Stuff the peppers with the meat-vegetable mixture.

5.   Place the peppers in the air fryer basket, set temperature to 360°F and bake for 9 to 13 minutes or until the filling is hot and the peppers are tender.

PER SERVING: CALORIES: 487; FAT: 21G; PROTEIN:26G; FIBER:6G

Pub Style Corned Beef Egg Rolls

Prep: 15 Minutes • Cook Time: 10 Minutes • Total: 35 Minutes
Serves: 10
Ingredients
Olive oil
½ C. orange marmalade
5 slices of Swiss cheese
4 C. corned beef and cabbage
1 egg
10 egg roll wrappers
Brandy Mustard Sauce:
1/16th tsp. pepper
2 tbsp. whole grain mustard
1 tsp. dry mustard powder
1 C. heavy cream
½ C. chicken stock
¼ C. brandy
¾ C. dry white wine
¼ tsp. curry powder
½ tbsp. cilantro
1 minced shallot
2 tbsp. ghee

Directions:
1.   To make mustard sauce, add shallots and ghee to skillet, cooking until softened. Then add brandy and wine, heating to a low boil. Cook 5 minutes for liquids to reduce. Add stock and seasonings. Simmer 5 minutes.
2.   Turn down heat and add heavy cream. Cook on low till sauce reduces and it covers the back of a spoon.
3.   Place sauce in the fridge to chill.
4.   Crack the egg in a bowl and set to the side.
5.   Lay out an egg wrapper with the corner towards you. Brush the edges with egg wash.
6.   Place 1/3 cup of corned beef mixture into the center along with 2 tablespoons of marmalade and ½ a slice of Swiss cheese.
7.   Fold the bottom corner over filling. As you are folding the sides, make sure they are stick well to the first flap you made.
8.   Place filled rolls into prepared air fryer basket. Spritz rolls with olive oil.
9.   Set temperature to 390°F, and set time to 10 minutes. Cook 10 minutes at 390 degrees, shaking halfway through cooking.
10.   Serve rolls with Brandy Mustard sauce.
PER SERVING: CALORIES: 415; FAT: 13G; PROTEIN:38G; SUGAR:4G

Stir-Fried Steak and Cabbage

Prep: 15 Minutes • Cook Time: 10 Minutes • Total: 35 Minutes
Serves: 4
Ingredients
½ pound sirloin steak, cut into strips
2 teaspoons cornstarch
1 tablespoon peanut oil
2 cups chopped red or green cabbage
1 yellow bell pepper, chopped
2 green onions, chopped
2 cloves garlic, sliced
½ cup commercial stir-fry sauce
Directions:
1. Toss the steak with the cornstarch and set aside.
2. In a 6-inch metal bowl, combine the peanut oil with the cabbage.
3. Place in the basket, set temperature to 360°F and cook for 3 to 4 minutes.
4. Remove the bowl from the basket and add the steak, pepper, onions, and garlic. Return to the air fryer oven and cook for 3 to 5 minutes or until the steak is cooked to desired doneness and vegetables are crisp and tender.
5. Add the stir-fry sauce and cook for 2 to 4 minutes or until hot. Serve over rice.

PER SERVING: CALORIES: 180; FAT: 7G; PROTEIN:20G; FIBER:2G

Reuben Egg Rolls

Prep: 5 Minutes • Cook Time: 20 Minutes • Total: 25 Minutes
Serves: 6
Ingredients
Swiss cheese
Can of sauerkraut
Sliced deli corned beef
Egg roll wrappers
Directions:
1. Cut corned beef and Swiss cheese into thin slices.
2. Drain sauerkraut and dry well.
3. Take egg roll wrapper and moisten edges with water.
4. Stack center with corned beef and cheese till you reach desired thickness. Top off with sauerkraut.
5. Fold corner closest to you over the edge of filling. Bring up sides and glue with water.
6. Add to the air fryer oven basket and spritz with olive oil.
7. Set temperature to 400°F, and set time to 4 minutes. Cook 4 minutes at 400 degrees, then flip and cook another 4 minutes.

PER SERVING: CALORIES: 251; FAT: 12G; PROTEIN:31G; SUGAR:4G

Air-Fried Philly Cheesesteak

Prep: 5 Minutes • Cook Time: 16 Minutes • Total: 21 Minutes
Serves: 6
Ingredients
Large hoagie bun, sliced in half
6 ounces of sirloin or flank steak, sliced into bite-sized pieces
½ white onion, rinsed and sliced
½ red pepper, rinsed and sliced
slices of American cheese
Directions:
1.   Set the air fryer oven to 320 degrees for 10 minutes.
2.   Arrange the steak pieces, onions and peppers on a piece of tin foil, flat and not overlapping, and set the tin foil on one side of the air-fryer basket. The foil should not take up more than half of the surface; the juices from the steak and the moisture from the vegetables will mingle while cooking.
3.   Lay the hoagie-bun halves, crusty-side up and soft-side down, on the other half of the air fryer.
4.   After 10 minutes, the air fryer will shut off; the hoagie buns should be starting to crisp and the steak and vegetables will have begun to cook.
5.   Carefully, flip the hoagie buns so they are now crusty-side down and soft-side up; cover both sides with one slice each of American cheese.
6.   With a long spoon, gently stir the steak, onions and peppers in the foil to ensure even coverage.
7.   Set the air fryer to 360 degrees for 6 minutes.
8.   After 6 minutes, when the fryer shuts off, the cheese will be perfectly melted over the toasted bread, and the steak will be juicy on the inside and crispy on the outside.
9.   Remove the cheesy hoagie halves first, using tongs, and set on a serving plate; then cover one side with the steak, and top with the onions and peppers. Close with the other cheesy hoagie-half, slice into two pieces, and enjoy.

Herbed Roast Beef

Prep: 5 Minutes • Cook Time: 20 Minutes • Total: 25 Minutes
Serves: 6
Ingredients
½ tsp. fresh rosemary
1 tsp. dried thyme
¼ tsp. pepper
1 tsp. salt
4-pound top round roast beef
tsp. olive oil
Directions:
1.   Ensure your air fryer oven is preheated to 360 degrees.
2.   Rub olive oil all over beef.
3.   Mix rosemary, thyme, pepper, and salt together and proceed to rub all sides of beef with spice mixture.
4.   Pour into the Oven rack/basket. Place the Rack on the middle-shelf of the Air fryer oven. Set temperature to 360°F, and set time to 20 minutes.
5.   Allow roast to rest 10 minutes before slicing to serve.
PER SERVING: CALORIES: 502; FAT: 18G; PROTEIN:48G; SUGAR:2G

Tender Beef with Sour Cream Sauce

Prep: 5 Minutes • Cook Time: 12 Minutes • Total: 17 Minutes
Serves: 2
Ingredients
9 ounces tender beef, chopped
1 cup scallions, chopped
2 cloves garlic, smashed
3/4 cup sour cream
3/4 teaspoon salt
1/4 teaspoon black pepper, or to taste
1/2 teaspoon dried dill weed
Directions:
1.   Add the beef, scallions, and garlic to the baking dish.
2.   Cook for about 5 minutes at 390 degrees F.
3.   Once the meat is starting to tender, pour in the sour cream. Stir in the salt, black pepper, and dill.
4.   Now, cook 7 minutes longer.

Beef Empanadas

Prep: 5 Minutes • Cook Time: 20 Minutes • Total: 25 Minutes
Serves: 6
Ingredients
1 tsp. water
1 egg white
1 C. picadillo
8 Goya empanada discs (thawed)
Directions:
1.   Ensure your air fryer oven is preheated to 325. Spray basket with olive oil.
2.   Place 2 tablespoons of picadillo into the center of each disc. Fold disc in half and use a fork to seal edges. Repeat with all ingredients.
3.   Whisk egg white with water and brush tops of empanadas with egg wash.
4.   Add 2-3 empanadas to the air fryer.
5.   Set temperature to 325°F, and set time to 8 minutes, cook until golden. Repeat till you cook all filled empanadas.
PER SERVING: CALORIES: 183; FAT: 5G; PROTEIN:11G; SUGAR:2G

Beef Pot Pie

Prep: 5 Minutes • Cook Time: 90 Minutes • Total: 95 Minutes
Serves: 2
Ingredients
1 tablespoon olive oil
1 pound beef stewing steak, cubed
1 large onion, chopped
1 tablespoon tomato puree
1 can ale
Warm water, as required
2 beef bouillon cubes
Salt and freshly ground black pepper, to taste
1 tablespoon plain flour plus more for dusting
1 prepared short crust pastry
Directions:
1. In a pan, heat oil on medium heat. Add steak and cook for about 4-5 minutes. Add onion and cook for about 4-5 minutes.
2. Add tomato puree and cook for about 2-3 minutes.
3. In a jug, add the ale and enough water to double the mixture.
4. Add the ale mixture, cubes, salt and black pepper in the pan with beef and bring to a boil on high heat. Reduce the heat to low and simmer for about 1 hour.
5. In a bowl, mix together flour and 3 tablespoons of warm water.
6. Slowly, add the flour mixture in beef mixture, stirring continuously.
7. Remove from heat and keep aside. Roll out the short crust pastry.
8. Line 2 ramekins with pastry and dust with flour.
9. Divide the beef mixture in the ramekins evenly.
10. Place extra pastry on top.
11. Preheat the air fryer oven to 390 degrees F, and Cook for about 10 minutes.
12. Now, set the air fryer oven to 335 degrees F, and Cook for about 6 minutes more.

Bolognaise Sauce

Prep: 5 Minutes • Cook Time: 30 Minutes • Total: 35 Minutes
Serves: 2
Ingredients
13 Ozs Ground Beef
1 Carrot
1 Stalk of Celery
10 Ozs Diced Tomatoes
1/2 Onion
Salt and Pepper to taste
Oven safe bowl
Directions:
1. Preheat the air fryer oven to 390 degrees.
2. Finely dice the carrot, celery and onions. Place into the oven safe bowl along with the ground beef and combine well
3. Place the bowl into the air fryer oven tray and cook for 12 minutes until browned.
4. Pour the diced tomatoes into the bowl and replace in the air fryer.
5. Season with salt and pepper, then cook for another 18 minutes
6. Serve over cooked pasta or freeze for later use.

Breaded Spam Steaks

Prep: 5 Minutes • Cook Time: 5 Minutes • Total: 10 Minutes
Serves: 2

Ingredients

12 Oz Can Luncheon Meat
1 Cup All Purpose Flour
2 Eggs, beaten
2 Cups Italian Seasoned Breadcrumbs

Directions:

1.   Preheat the air fryer oven to 380 degrees.
2.   Cut the luncheon meat into 1/4 inch slices.
3.   Gently press the luncheon meat slices into the flour to coat and shake off the excess flour. Dip into the beaten egg, then press into breadcrumbs.
4.   Place the battered slices into the air fryer tray and cook for 3 to 5 minutes until golden brown.
5.   Serve with chili or tomato sauce

Air Fryer Burgers

Prep: 5 Minutes • Cook Time: 10 Minutes • Total: 15 Minutes
Serves: 4

Ingredients

1 pound lean ground beef
1 tsp. dried parsley
½ tsp. dried oregano
½ tsp. pepper
½ tsp. salt
½ tsp. onion powder
½ tsp. garlic powder
Few drops of liquid smoke
1 tsp. Worcestershire sauce

Directions:

1.   Ensure your air fryer oven is preheated to 350 degrees.
2.   Mix all seasonings together till combined.
3.   Place beef in a bowl and add seasonings. Mix well, but do not overmix.
4.   Make 4 patties from the mixture and using your thumb, making an indent in the center of each patty.
5.   Add patties to air fryer basket.
6.   Set temperature to 350°F, and set time to 10 minutes, and cook 10 minutes. No need to turn.

PER SERVING: CALORIES: 148; FAT: 5G; PROTEIN:24G; SUGAR:1G

Cheese-Stuffed Meatballs

Prep: 10 Minutes • Cook Time: 10 Minutes • Total: 20 Minutes
Serves: 4

Ingredients

⅓ cup soft bread crumbs
3 tablespoons milk
1 tablespoon ketchup
1 egg
½ teaspoon dried marjoram
Pinch salt
Freshly ground black pepper
1 pound 95 percent lean ground beef
20 ½-inch cubes of cheese
Olive oil for misting

Directions:

1.   In a large bowl, combine the bread crumbs, milk, ketchup, egg, marjoram, salt, and pepper, and mix well. Add the ground beef and mix gently but thoroughly with your hands. Form the mixture into 20 meatballs. Shape each meatball around a cheese cube. Mist the meatballs with olive oil and put into the air fryer oven basket.
2.   Bake for 10 to 13 minutes or until the meatballs register 165°F on a meat thermometer.

PER SERVING: CALORIES: 393; FAT: 17G; PROTEIN:50G; FIBER:0G

Roasted Stuffed Peppers

Prep: 5 Minutes • Cook Time: 20 Minutes • Total: 25 Minutes
Serves: 4
Ingredients
4 ounces shredded cheddar cheese
½ tsp. pepper
½ tsp. salt
1 tsp. Worcestershire sauce
½ C. tomato sauce
8 ounces lean ground beef
1 tsp. olive oil
1 minced garlic clove
½ chopped onion
2 green peppers
Directions:
1.   Ensure your air fryer is preheated to 390 degrees. Spray with olive oil.
2.   Cut stems off bell peppers and remove seeds. Cook in boiling salted water for 3 minutes.
3.   Sauté garlic and onion together in a skillet until golden in color.
4.   Take skillet off the heat. Mix pepper, salt, Worcestershire sauce, ¼ cup of tomato sauce, half of cheese and beef together.
5.   Divide meat mixture into pepper halves. Top filled peppers with remaining cheese and tomato sauce.
6.   Place filled peppers in the air fryer oven.
7.   Set temperature to 390°F, and set time to 20 minutes, bake 15-20 minutes.
PER SERVING: CALORIES: 295; FAT: 8G; PROTEIN:23G; SUGAR:2G

Air Fried Steak Sandwich

Prep: 5 Minutes • Cook Time: 16 Minutes • Total: 21 Minutes
Serves: 4
Ingredients
Large hoagie bun, sliced in half
6 ounces of sirloin or flank steak, sliced into bite-sized pieces
½ tablespoon of mustard powder
½ tablespoon of soy sauce
1 tablespoon of fresh bleu cheese, crumbled
8 medium-sized cherry tomatoes, sliced in half
1 cup of fresh arugula, rinsed and patted dry
Directions:
1.   In a small mixing bowl, combine the soy sauce and onion powder; stir with a fork until thoroughly combined.
2.   Lay the raw steak strips in the soy-mustard mixture, and fully immerse each piece to marinate.
3.   Set the air fryer oven to 320 degrees for 10 minutes.
4.   Arrange the soy-mustard marinated steak pieces on a piece of tin foil, flat and not overlapping, and set the tin foil on one side of the air fryer basket. The foil should not take up more than half of the surface.
5.   Lay the hoagie-bun halves, crusty-side up and soft-side down, on the other half of the air fryer oven.
6.   After 10 minutes, the air fryer oven will shut off; the hoagie buns should be starting to crisp and the steak will have begun to cook.
7.   Carefully, flip the hoagie buns so they are now crusty-side down and soft-side up; crumble a layer of the bleu cheese on each hoagie half.
8.   With a long spoon, gently stir the marinated steak in the foil to ensure even coverage.
9.   Set the air fryer to 360 degrees for 6 minutes.
10.   After 6 minutes, when the fryer shuts off, the bleu cheese will be perfectly melted over the toasted bread, and the steak will be juicy on the inside and crispy on the outside.
11.   Remove the cheesy hoagie halves first, using tongs, and set on a serving plate; then cover one side with the steak, and top with the cherry-tomato halves and the arugula. Close with the other cheesy hoagie-half, slice into two pieces, and enjoy.

Carrot and Beef Cocktail Balls

Prep: 5 Minutes • Cook Time: 20 Minutes • Total: 25 Minutes
Serves: 10
Ingredients
1 pound ground beef
2 carrots
1 red onion, peeled and chopped
2 cloves garlic
1/2 teaspoon dried rosemary, crushed
1/2 teaspoon dried basil
1 teaspoon dried oregano
1 egg
3/4 cup breadcrumbs
1/2 teaspoon salt
1/2 teaspoon black pepper, or to taste
1 cup plain flour
Directions:
1.   Place ground beef in a large bowl. In a food processor, pulse the carrot, onion and garlic; transfer the vegetable mixture to a large-sized bowl.
2.   Then, add the rosemary, basil, oregano, egg, breadcrumbs, salt, and black pepper.
3.   Shape the mixture into even balls; refrigerate for about 30 minutes. Roll the balls into the flour.
4.   Pour the balls into the Oven rack/basket. Place the Rack on the middle-shelf of the Air fryer oven. Set temperature to 350°F, and set time to 20 minutes, turning occasionally; work with batches. Serve with toothpicks.

Beef Steaks with Beans

Prep: 5 Minutes • Cook Time: 10 Minutes • Total: 15 Minutes
Serves: 4
Ingredients
4 beef steaks, trim the fat and cut into strips
1 cup green onions, chopped
2 cloves garlic, minced
1 red bell pepper, seeded and thinly sliced
1 can tomatoes, crushed
1 can cannellini beans
3/4 cup beef broth
1/4 teaspoon dried basil
1/2 teaspoon cayenne pepper
1/2 teaspoon sea salt
1/4 teaspoon ground black pepper, or to taste
Directions:
1.   Add the steaks, green onions and garlic to the air fryer oven basket.
2.   Cook at 390 degrees F for 10 minutes, working in batches.
3.   Stir in the remaining ingredients and cook for an additional 5 minutes.

Air Fryer Beef Steak

Prep: 5 Minutes • Cook Time: 15 Minutes • Total: 20 Minutes
Serves: 4
Ingredients
1 tbsp. olive oil
Pepper and salt
2 pounds of ribeye steak
Directions:
1.   Season meat on both sides with pepper and salt.
2.   Rub all sides of meat with olive oil.
3.   Preheat air fryer oven to 356 degrees and spritz with olive oil.
4.   Pour into the Oven rack/basket. Place the Rack on the middle-shelf of the Air fryer oven. Set temperature to 356°F, and set time to 7 minutes. Flip and cook an additional 6 minutes.
5.   Let meat sit 2-5 minutes to rest. Slice and serve with salad.
PER SERVING: CALORIES: 233; FAT: 19G; PROTEIN:16G; SUGAR:0G

Mushroom Meatloaf

Prep: 5 Minutes • Cook Time: 25 Minutes • Total: 30 Minutes
Serves: 4
Ingredients
14-ounce lean ground beef
1 chorizo sausage, chopped finely
1 small onion, chopped
1 garlic clove, minced
2 tablespoons fresh cilantro, chopped
3 tablespoons breadcrumbs
1 egg
Salt and freshly ground black pepper, to taste
2 tablespoons fresh mushrooms, sliced thinly
3 tablespoons olive oil
Directions:
1.   Preheat the Air fryer oven to 390 degrees F.
2.   In a large bowl, add all ingredients except mushrooms and mix till well combined.
3.   In a baking pan, place the beef mixture.
4.   With the back of spatula, smooth the surface.
5.   Top with mushroom slices and gently, press into the meatloaf.
6.   Drizzle with oil evenly.
7.   Arrange the pan in the air fryer oven basket and cook for about 25 minutes.
8.   Cut the meatloaf in desires size wedges and serve.

Beef and Broccoli

Prep: 10 Minutes • Cook Time: 12 Minutes • Total: 25 Minutes

Serves: 4

Ingredients

1 minced garlic clove
1 sliced ginger root
1 tbsp. olive oil
1 tsp. almond flour
1 tsp. sweetener of choice
1 tsp. low-sodium soy sauce
1/3 C. sherry
2 tsp. sesame oil
1/3 C. oyster sauce
1 pounds of broccoli
¾ pound round steak

Directions:

1.   Remove stems from broccoli and slice into florets. Slice steak into thin strips.
2.   Combine sweetener, soy sauce, sherry, almond flour, sesame oil, and oyster sauce together, stirring till sweetener dissolves.
3.   Put strips of steak into the mixture and allow to marinate 45 minutes to 2 hours.
4.   Add broccoli and marinated steak to air fryer basket. Place garlic, ginger, and olive oil on top.
5.   Set temperature to 400°F, and set time to 12 minutes. Cook 12 minutes at 400 degrees. Serve with cauliflower rice!

PER SERVING: CALORIES: 384; FAT: 16G; PROTEIN:19G; SUGAR:4G

Air Fryer Beef Fajitas

Prep: 5 Minutes • Cook Time: 20 Minutes • Total: 25 Minutes

Serves: 6

Ingredients

Beef:
1/8 C. carne asada seasoning
2 pounds beef flap meat
Diet 7-Up
Fajita veggies:
1 tsp. chili powder
1-2 tsp. pepper
1-2 tsp. salt
2 bell peppers, your choice of color
1 onion

Directions:

1.   Slice flap meat into manageable pieces and place into a bowl. Season meat with carne seasoning and pour diet soda over meat. Cover and chill overnight.
2.   Ensure your air fryer is preheated to 380 degrees.
3.   Place a parchment liner into the air fryer oven basket and spray with olive oil. Place beef in layers into the basket.
4.   Cook 8-10 minutes, making sure to flip halfway through. Remove and set to the side.
5.   Slice up veggies and spray air fryer basket. Add veggies to the fryer and spray with olive oil.
6.   Set temperature to 400°F, and set time to 10 minutes. Cook 10 minutes at 400 degrees, shaking 1-2 times during cooking process.
7.   Serve meat and veggies on wheat tortillas and top with favorite keto fillings.

PER SERVING: CALORIES: 412; FAT: 21G; PROTEIN:13G; SUGAR:1G

Seafood Recipes

Coconut Shrimp

Prep: 5 Minutes • Cook Time: 10 Minutes • Total: 15 Minutes
Serves: 3
Ingredients
1 C. almond flour
1 C. panko breadcrumbs
1 tbsp. coconut flour
1 C. unsweetened, dried coconut
1 egg white
12 raw large shrimp
Directions:
1.   Put shrimp on paper towels to drain.
2.   Mix coconut and panko breadcrumbs together. Then mix in coconut flour and almond flour in a different bowl. Set to the side.
3.   Dip shrimp into flour mixture, then into egg white, and then into coconut mixture.
4.   Place into air fryer basket. Repeat with remaining shrimp.
5.   Set temperature to 350°F, and set time to 10 minutes. Turn halfway through cooking process.
PER SERVING: CALORIES:213; FAT: 8G; PROTEIN:15G; SUGAR:3G

Grilled Salmon

Prep: 5 Minutes • Cook Time: 10 Minutes • Total: 15 Minutes
Serves: 3
Ingredients
2 Salmon Fillets
1/2 Tsp Lemon Pepper
1/2 Tsp Garlic Powder
Salt and Pepper
1/3 Cup Soy Sauce
1/3 Cup Sugar
1 Tbsp Olive Oil
Directions:
1.   Season salmon fillets with lemon pepper, garlic powder and salt. In a shallow bowl, add a third cup of water and combine the olive oil, soy sauce and sugar. Place salmon the bowl and immerse in the sauce. Cover with cling film and allow to marinate in the refrigerator for at least an hour.
2.   Preheat the air fryer oven at 350 degrees.
3.   Place salmon into the air fryer and cook for 10 minutes or more until the fish is tender.
4.   Serve with lemon wedges

Bacon Wrapped Shrimp

Prep: 5 Minutes • Cook Time: 5 Minutes • Total: 10 Minutes
Serves: 4
Ingredients
1¼ pound tiger shrimp, peeled and deveined
1 pound bacon
Directions:
1.   Wrap each shrimp with a slice of bacon.
2.   Refrigerate for about 20 minutes.
3.   Preheat the air fryer oven to 390 degrees F.
4.   Arrange the shrimp in the air fryer basket.
5.   Cook for about 5-7 minutes.

Crispy Paprika Fish Fillets

Prep: 5 Minutes • Cook Time: 15 Minutes • Total: 20 Minutes
Serves: 4
Ingredients
1/2 cup seasoned breadcrumbs
1 tablespoon balsamic vinegar
1/2 teaspoon seasoned salt
1 teaspoon paprika
1/2 teaspoon ground black pepper
1 teaspoon celery seed
2 fish fillets, halved
1 egg, beaten
Directions:
1.   Add the breadcrumbs, vinegar, salt, paprika, ground black pepper, and celery seeds to your food processor. Process for about 30 seconds.
2.   Coat the fish fillets with the beaten egg; then, coat them with the breadcrumbs mixture.
3.   Pour into the Oven rack/basket. Place the Rack on the middle-shelf of the Air fryer oven. Set temperature to 350°F, and set time to 15 minutes.

Air Fryer Salmon

Prep: 5 Minutes • Cook Time: 10 Minutes • Total: 15 Minutes
Serves: 2
Ingredients
½ tsp. salt
½ tsp. garlic powder
½ tsp. smoked paprika
Salmon
Directions:
1.   Mix spices together and sprinkle onto salmon.
2.   Place seasoned salmon into the air fryer oven.
3.   Pour into the Oven rack/basket. Place the Rack on the middle-shelf of the Air fryer oven. Set temperature to 400°F, and set time to 10 minutes.
PER SERVING: CALORIES: 185; FAT: 11G; PROTEIN:21G; SUGAR:0G

Steamed Salmon & Sauce

Prep: 5 Minutes • Cook Time: 10 Minutes • Total: 15 Minutes
Serves: 2
Ingredients
1 cup Water
2 x 6 oz Fresh Salmon
2 Tsp Vegetable Oil
A Pinch of Salt for Each Fish
½ cup Plain Greek Yogurt
½ cup Sour Cream
2 Tbsp Finely Chopped Dill (Keep a bit for garnishing)
A Pinch of Salt to Taste
Directions:
1.   Pour the water into the tray of the air fryer oven and start heating to 285° F.
2.   Drizzle oil over the fish and spread it. Salt the fish to taste.
3.   Now pop it into the air fryer oven for 10 min.
4.   In the meantime, mix the yogurt, cream, dill and a bit of salt to make the sauce. When the fish is done, serve with the sauce and garnish with sprigs of dill..

Indian Fish Fingers

Prep: 35 Minutes • Cook Time: 15 Minutes • Total: 50 Minutes
Serves: 4
Ingredients
1/2 pound fish fillet
1 tablespoon finely chopped fresh mint leaves or any fresh herbs
1/3 cup bread crumbs
1 teaspoon ginger garlic paste or ginger and garlic powders
1 hot green chili finely chopped
1/2 teaspoon paprika
Generous pinch of black pepper
Salt to taste
3/4 tablespoons lemon juice
3/4 teaspoons garam masala powder
1/3 teaspoon rosemary
1 egg
Directions:
1.   Start by removing any skin on the fish, washing, and patting dry. Cut the fish into fingers.
2.   In a medium bowl mix together all ingredients except for fish, mint, and bread crumbs. Bury the fingers in the mixture and refrigerate for 30 minutes.
3.   Remove from the bowl from the fridge and mix in mint leaves.
4.   In a separate bowl beat the egg, pour bread crumbs into a third bowl. Dip the fingers in the egg bowl then toss them in the bread crumbs bowl.
5.   Pour into the Oven rack/basket. Place the Rack on the middle-shelf of the Air fryer oven. Set temperature to 360°F, and set time to 15 minutes, toss the fingers halfway through.
PER SERVING: CALORIES: 187; FAT: 7G; PROTEIN:11G; FIBER:1G

Healthy Fish and Chips

Prep: 5 Minutes • Cook Time: 15 Minutes • Total: 20 Minutes
Serves: 3
Ingredients
Old Bay seasoning
½ C. panko breadcrumbs
1 egg
2 tbsp. almond flour
4-6 ounce tilapia fillets
Frozen crinkle cut fries
Directions:
1.   Add almond flour to one bowl, beat egg in another bowl, and add panko breadcrumbs to the third bowl, mixed with Old Bay seasoning.
2.   Dredge tilapia in flour, then egg, and then breadcrumbs.
3.   Place coated fish in air fryer oven along with fries.
4.   Set temperature to 390°F, and set time to 15 minutes.
PER SERVING: CALORIES: 219; FAT: 5G; PROTEIN:25G; SUGAR:1G

Quick Paella

Prep: 7 Minutes • Cook Time: 15 Minutes • Total: 22 Minutes
Serves: 4

Ingredients

1 (10-ounce) package frozen cooked rice, thawed
1 (6-ounce) jar artichoke hearts, drained and chopped
¼ cup vegetable broth
½ teaspoon turmeric
½ teaspoon dried thyme
1 cup frozen cooked small shrimp
½ cup frozen baby peas
1 tomato, diced

Directions:

1.   In a 6-by-6-by-2-inch pan, combine the rice, artichoke hearts, vegetable broth, turmeric, and thyme, and stir gently.

2.   Place in the air fryer oven, set temperature to 390°F and bake for 8 to 9 minutes or until the rice is hot. Remove from the air fryer and gently stir in the shrimp, peas, and tomato. Cook for 5 to 8 minutes or until the shrimp and peas are hot and the paella is bubbling.

PER SERVING: CALORIES: 345; FAT: 1G; PROTEIN:18G; FIBER:4G

Coconut Shrimp

Prep: 15 Minutes • Cook Time: 5 Minutes • Total: 20 Minutes
Serves: 4

Ingredients

1 (8-ounce) can crushed pineapple
½ cup sour cream
¼ cup pineapple preserves
2 egg whites
⅔ cup cornstarch
⅔ cup sweetened coconut
1 cup panko bread crumbs
1 pound uncooked large shrimp, thawed if frozen, deveined and shelled
Olive oil for misting

Directions:

1.   Drain the crushed pineapple well, reserving the juice. In a small bowl, combine the pineapple, sour cream, and preserves, and mix well. Set aside. In a shallow bowl, beat the egg whites with 2 tablespoons of the reserved pineapple liquid. Place the cornstarch on a plate. Combine the coconut and bread crumbs on another plate. Dip the shrimp into the cornstarch, shake it off, then dip into the egg white mixture and finally into the coconut mixture. Place the shrimp in the air fryer basket and mist with oil.

2.   Set temperature to 390°F. Cook for 5 to 7 minutes or until the shrimp are crisp and golden brown

PER SERVING: CALORIES: 524; FAT: 14G; PROTEIN:33G; FIBER:4G

3-Ingredient Air Fryer Catfish

Prep: 5 Minutes • Cook Time: 13 Minutes • Total: 20 Minutes
Serves: 4
Ingredients
1 tbsp. chopped parsley
1 tbsp. olive oil
¼ C. seasoned fish fry
4 catfish fillets
Directions:
1.   Ensure your air fryer oven is preheated to 400 degrees.
2.   Rinse off catfish fillets and pat dry.
3.   Add fish fry seasoning to Ziploc baggie, then catfish. Shake bag and ensure fish gets well coated.
4.   Spray each fillet with olive oil.
5.   Add fillets to air fryer basket.
6.   Set temperature to 400°F, and set time to 10 minutes.
7.   Cook 10 minutes. Then flip and cook another 2-3 minutes.
PER SERVING: CALORIES: 208; FAT: 5G; PROTEIN:17G; SUGAR:0.5G

Tuna Veggie Stir-Fry

Prep: 5 Minutes • Cook Time: 12 Minutes • Total: 17 Minutes
Serves: 4
Ingredients
1 tablespoon olive oil
1 red bell pepper, chopped
1 cup green beans, cut into 2-inch pieces
1 onion, sliced
2 cloves garlic, sliced
2 tablespoons low-sodium soy sauce
1 tablespoon honey
½ pound fresh tuna, cubed
Directions:
1.   In a 6-inch metal bowl, combine the olive oil, pepper, green beans, onion, and garlic.
2.   Pour into the Oven rack/basket. Place the Rack on the middle-shelf of the Air fryer oven. Set temperature to 350°F, and set time to 4 to 6 minutes, stirring once, until crisp and tender. Add soy sauce, honey, and tuna, and stir. Cook for another 3 to 6 minutes, stirring once, until the tuna is cooked as desired. Tuna can be served rare or medium-rare, or you can cook it until well done.
PER SERVING: CALORIES: 187; FAT: 8G; PROTEIN:17G; FIBER:2G

Salmon Quiche

Prep: 5 Minutes • Cook Time: 12 Minutes • Total: 17 Minutes
Serves: 4
Ingredients
5 Ozs Salmon Fillet
1/2 Tbsp Lemon Juice
1/2 Cup Flour
1/4 Cup Butter, melted
2 Eggs and 1 Egg Yolk
3 Tbsps Whipped Cream
Tsps Mustard
Black Pepper to taste
Salt and Pepper
* Quiche Pan
Directions:
1.   Clean and cut the salmon into small cubes.
2.   Heat the air fryer oven to 375 degrees
3.   Pour the lemon juice over the salmon cubes and allow to marinate for an hour.
4.   Combine a tablespoon of water with the butter, flour and yolk in a large bowl. Using your hands, knead the mixture until smooth
5.   On a clean surface, use a rolling pin to form a circle of dough. Place this into the quiche pan, using your fingers to adhere the pastry to the edges
6.   Whisk the cream, mustard and eggs together. Season with salt and pepper. Add the marinated salmon into the bowl and combine.
7.   Pour the content of the bowl into the dough lined quiche pan
8.   Put the pan in the air fryer oven tray and cook for 25 minutes until browned and crispy.

Cilantro-Lime Fried Shrimp

Prep: 10 Minutes • Cook Time: 10 Minutes • Total: 20 Minutes
Serves: 4
Ingredients
1 pound raw shrimp, peeled and deveined with tails on or off (see Prep tip)
½ cup chopped fresh cilantro
Juice of 1 lime
1 egg
½ cup all-purpose flour
¾ cup bread crumbs
Salt
Pepper
Cooking oil
½ cup cocktail sauce (optional)
Directions:
1.   Place the shrimp in a plastic bag and add the cilantro and lime juice. Seal the bag. Shake to combine. Marinate in the refrigerator for 30 minutes.
2.   In a small bowl, beat the egg. In another small bowl, place the flour. Place the bread crumbs in a third small bowl, and season with salt and pepper to taste.
3.   Spray the air fryer basket with cooking oil.
4.   Remove the shrimp from the plastic bag. Dip each in the flour, then the egg, and then the bread crumbs.
5.   Place the shrimp in the air fryer oven. It is okay to stack them. Spray the shrimp with cooking oil. Set temperature to 360°F. Cook for 4 minutes.
6.   Open the air fryer and flip the shrimp. I recommend flipping individually instead of shaking to keep the breading intact. Cook for an additional 4 minutes, or until crisp.
7.   Cool before serving. Serve with cocktail sauce if desired.
PER SERVING: CALORIES: 254; FAT:4G; PROTEIN:29G; FIBER:1G

Lemony Tuna

Prep: 10 Minutes • Cook Time: 10 Minutes • Total: 20 Minutes
Serves: 4
Ingredients
2 (6-ounce) cans water packed plain tuna
2 teaspoons Dijon mustard
½ cup breadcrumbs
1 tablespoon fresh lime juice
2 tablespoons fresh parsley, chopped
1 egg
air fryer of hot sauce
3 tablespoons canola oil
Salt and freshly ground black pepper, to taste
Directions:
1.   Drain most of the liquid from the canned tuna.
2.   In a bowl, add the fish, mustard, crumbs, citrus juice, parsley and hot sauce and mix till well combined. Add a little canola oil if it seems too dry. Add egg, salt and stir to combine. Make the patties from tuna mixture. Refrigerate the tuna patties for about 2 hours.
3.   Pour into the Oven rack/basket. Place the Rack on the middle-shelf of the Air fryer oven. Set temperature to 355°F, and set time to 12 minutes.

Bang Panko Breaded Fried Shrimp

Prep: 5 Minutes • Cook Time: 8 Minutes • Total: 13 Minutes
Serves: 4
Ingredients
1 tsp. paprika
Montreal chicken seasoning
¾ C. panko bread crumbs
½ C. almond flour
1 egg white
1 pound raw shrimp (peeled and deveined)
Bang Bang Sauce:
¼ C. sweet chili sauce
2 tbsp. sriracha sauce
1/3 C. plain Greek yogurt
Directions:
1.   Ensure your air fryer oven is preheated to 400 degrees.
2.   Season all shrimp with seasonings.
3.   Add flour to one bowl, egg white in another, and breadcrumbs to a third.
4.   Dip seasoned shrimp in flour, then egg whites, and then breadcrumbs.
5.   Spray coated shrimp with olive oil and add to air fryer basket.
6.   Set temperature to 400°F, and set time to 4 minutes. Cook 4 minutes, flip, and cook an additional 4 minutes.
7.   To make the sauce, mix together all sauce ingredients until smooth.
PER SERVING: CALORIES: 212; CARBS:12; FAT: 1G; PROTEIN:37G; SUGAR:0.5G

Grilled Soy Salmon Fillets

PREP: 5 MINUTES • COOK TIME: 8 MINUTES • TOTAL: 13 MINUTES
SERVES: 4
Ingredients
4 salmon fillets
1/4 teaspoon ground black pepper
1/2 teaspoon cayenne pepper
1/2 teaspoon salt
1 teaspoon onion powder
1 tablespoon fresh lemon juice
1/2 cup soy sauce
1/2 cup water
1 tablespoon honey
2 tablespoons extra-virgin olive oil
Directions:
1.   Firstly, pat the salmon fillets dry using kitchen towels. Season the salmon with black pepper, cayenne pepper, salt, and onion powder.
2.   To make the marinade, combine together the lemon juice, soy sauce, water, honey, and olive oil. Marinate the salmon for at least 2 hours in your refrigerator.
3.   Arrange the fish fillets on a grill basket in your air fryer oven.
4.   Bake at 330 degrees for 8 to 9 minutes, or until salmon fillets are easily flaked with a fork.
5.   Work with batches and serve warm.

Flying Fish

Prep: 5 Minutes • Cook Time: 12 Minutes • Total: 17 Minutes
Serves: 6
Ingredients
4 Tbsp Oil
3–4 oz Breadcrumbs
1 Whisked Whole Egg in a Saucer/Soup Plate
4 Fresh Fish Fillets
Fresh Lemon (For serving)
Directions:
1.   Preheat the air fryer to 350° F. Mix the crumbs and oil until it looks nice and loose.
2.   Dip the fish in the egg and coat lightly, then move on to the crumbs. Make sure the fillet is covered evenly.
3.   Cook in the air fryer oven basket for roughly 12 minutes – depending on the size of the fillets you are using.
4.   Serve with fresh lemon & chips to complete the duo.

Pistachio-Crusted Lemon-Garlic Salmon

Prep: 5 Minutes • Cook Time: 20 Minutes • Total: 25 Minutes
Serves: 6
Ingredients
4 medium-sized salmon filets
2 raw eggs
3 ounces of melted butter
1 clove of garlic, peeled and finely minced
1 large-sized lemon
1 teaspoon of salt
1 tablespoon of parsley, rinsed, patted dry and chopped
1 teaspoon of dill, rinsed, patted dry and chopped
½ cup of pistachio nuts, shelled and coarsely crushed

Directions:
1.   Cover the basket of the air fryer with a lining of tin foil, leaving the edges uncovered to allow air to circulate through the basket.
2.   Preheat the air fryer oven to 350 degrees.
3.   In a mixing bowl, beat the eggs until fluffy and until the yolks and whites are fully combined.
4.   Add the melted butter, the juice of the lemon, the minced garlic, the parsley and the dill to the beaten eggs, and stir thoroughly.
5.   One by one, dunk the salmon filets into the wet mixture, then roll them in the crushed pistachios, coating completely.
6.   Place the coated salmon fillets in the air fryer oven basket.
7.   Set the air fryer oven timer for 10 minutes.
8.   When the air fryer shuts off, after 10 minutes, the salmon will be partly cooked and the crust beginning to crisp. Using tongs, turn each of the fish filets over.
9.   Reset the air fryer oven to 350 degrees for another 10 minutes.
10.   After 10 minutes, when the air fryer shuts off, the salmon will be perfectly cooked and the pistachio crust will be toasted and crispy. Using tongs, remove from the air fryer and serve.

Louisiana Shrimp Po Boy

Prep: 10 Minutes • Cook Time: 10 Minutes • Total: 20 Minutes
Serves: 6
Ingredients
1 tsp. creole seasoning
8 slices of tomato
Lettuce leaves
¼ C. buttermilk
½ C. Louisiana Fish Fry
1 pound deveined shrimp
Remoulade sauce:
1 chopped green onion
1 tsp. hot sauce
1 tsp. Dijon mustard
½ tsp. creole seasoning
1 tsp. Worcestershire sauce
Juice of ½ a lemon
½ C. vegan mayo
Directions:
1.   To make the sauce, combine all sauce ingredients until well incorporated. Chill while you cook shrimp.
2.   Mix seasonings together and liberally season shrimp.
3.   Add buttermilk to a bowl. Dip each shrimp into milk and place in a Ziploc bag. Chill half an hour to marinate.
4.   Add fish fry to a bowl. Take shrimp from marinating bag and dip into fish fry, then add to air fryer.
5.   Ensure your air fryer is preheated to 400 degrees.
6.   Spray shrimp with olive oil.
7.   Pour into the Oven rack/basket. Place the Rack on the middle-shelf of the Air fryer oven. Set temperature to 400°F, and set time to 5 minutes. Cook 5 minutes, flip and then cook another 5 minutes. Assemble "Keto" Po Boy by adding sauce to lettuce leaves, along with shrimp and tomato.
PER SERVING: CALORIES: 337; CARBS:5.5; FAT: 12G; PROTEIN:24G; SUGAR:2G

Old Bay Crab Cakes

Prep: 10 Minutes • Cook Time: 20 Minutes • Total: 30 Minutes
Serves: 4
Ingredients
slices dried bread, crusts removed
Small amount of milk
1 tablespoon mayonnaise
1 tablespoon Worcestershire sauce
1 tablespoon baking powder
1 tablespoon parsley flakes
1 teaspoon Old Bay® Seasoning
1/4 teaspoon salt
1 egg
1 pound lump crabmeat
Directions:
1.   Crush your bread over a large bowl until it is broken down into small pieces. Add milk and stir until bread crumbs are moistened. Mix in mayo and Worcestershire sauce. Add remaining ingredients and mix well. Shape into 4 patties.
2.   Pour into the Oven rack/basket. Place the Rack on the middle-shelf of the Air fryer oven. Set temperature to 360°F, and set time to 20 minutes, flip half way through.
PER SERVING: CALORIES: 165; CARBS:5.8; FAT: 4.5G; PROTEIN:24G; FIBER:0G

Scallops and Spring Veggies

Prep: 10 Minutes • Cook Time: 8 Minutes • Total: 18 Minutes
Serves: 4
Ingredients
½ pound asparagus, ends trimmed, cut into 2-inch pieces
1 cup sugar snap peas
1 pound sea scallops
1 tablespoon lemon juice
2 teaspoons olive oil
½ teaspoon dried thyme
Pinch salt
Freshly ground black pepper
Directions:
1.   Place the asparagus and sugar snap peas in the air fryer basket.
2.   Cook for 2 to 3 minutes or until the vegetables are just starting to get tender.
3.   Meanwhile, check the scallops for a small muscle attached to the side, and pull it off and discard.
4.   In a medium bowl, toss the scallops with the lemon juice, olive oil, thyme, salt, and pepper. Place into the air fryer oven basket on top of the vegetables.
5.   Set temperature to 350°F. Steam for 5 to 7 minutes, tossing the basket once during cooking time, until the scallops are just firm when tested with your finger and are opaque in the center, and the vegetables are tender. Serve immediately.
PER SERVING: CALORIES: 162; CARBS:10G; FAT: 4G; PROTEIN:22G; FIBER:3G

Air Fryer Salmon Patties

Prep: 8 Minutes • Cook Time: 7 Minutes • Total: 15 Minutes
Serves: 4
Ingredients
1 tbsp. olive oil
1 tbsp. ghee
¼ tsp. salt
1/8 tsp. pepper
1 egg
1 C. almond flour
1 can wild Alaskan pink salmon
Directions:
1.   Drain can of salmon into a bowl and keep liquid. Discard skin and bones.
2.   Add salt, pepper, and egg to salmon, mixing well with hands to incorporate. Make patties.
3.   Dredge in flour and remaining egg. If it seems dry, spoon reserved salmon liquid from the can onto patties.
4.   Pour the patties into the Oven rack/basket. Place the Rack on the middle-shelf of the Air fryer oven. Set temperature to 378°F, and set time to 7 minutes. Cook 7 minutes till golden, making sure to flip once during cooking process.
PER SERVING: CALORIES: 437; CARBS:55; FAT: 12G; PROTEIN:24G; SUGAR:2G

Salmon Noodles

Prep: 5 Minutes • Cook Time: 16 Minutes • Total: 21 Minutes
Serves: 4
Ingredients
1 Salmon Fillet
1 Tbsp Teriyaki Marinade
3 ½ Ozs Soba Noodles, cooked and drained
10 Ozs Firm Tofu
7 Ozs Mixed Salad
1 Cup Broccoli
Olive Oil
Salt and Pepper to taste
Directions:
1.   Season the salmon with salt and pepper to taste, then coat with the teriyaki marinate. Set aside for 15 minutes
2.   Preheat the air fryer oven at 350 degrees, then cook the salmon for 8 minutes.
3.   Whilst the air fryer is cooking the salmon, start slicing the tofu into small cubes.
4.   Next, slice the broccoli into smaller chunks. Drizzle with olive oil.
5.   Once the salmon is cooked, put the broccoli and tofu into the air fryer oven tray for 8 minutes.
6.   Plate the salmon and broccoli tofu mixture over the soba noodles. Add the mixed salad to the side and serve.

Beer-Battered Fish and Chips

Prep: 5 Minutes • Cook Time: 30 Minutes • Total: 35 Minutes
Serves: 4
Ingredients
2 eggs
1 cup malty beer, such as Pabst Blue Ribbon
1 cup all-purpose flour
½ cup cornstarch
1 teaspoon garlic powder
Salt
Pepper
Cooking oil
(4-ounce) cod fillets
Directions:
1 In a medium bowl, beat the eggs with the beer. In another medium bowl, combine the flour and cornstarch, and season with the garlic powder and salt and pepper to taste.
Spray the air fryer basket with cooking oil.
Dip each cod fillet in the flour and cornstarch mixture and then in the egg and beer mixture. Dip the cod in the flour and cornstarch a second time.
2 Place the cod in the air fryer oven. Do not stack. Cook in batches. Spray with cooking oil. Set temperature to 390°F and cook for 8 minutes.
Open the air fryer oven and flip the cod. Cook for an additional 7 minutes.
Remove the cooked cod from the air fryer, then repeat steps 4 and 5 for the remaining fillets.
Serve with prepared air fried frozen fries. Frozen fries will need to be cooked for 18 to 20 minutes at 400ºF. Cool before serving.
PER SERVING: CALORIES: 325; CARBS:41; FAT: 4G; PROTEIN:26G; FIBER:1G

Tuna Stuffed Potatoes

Prep: 5 Minutes • Cook Time: 30 Minutes • Total: 35 Minutes
Serves: 4
Ingredients
4 starchy potatoes
½ tablespoon olive oil
1 (6-ounce) can tuna, drained
2 tablespoons plain Greek yogurt
1 teaspoon red chili powder
Salt and freshly ground black pepper, to taste
1 scallion, chopped and divided
1 tablespoon capers
Directions:
1.	In a large bowl of water, soak the potatoes for about 30 minutes. Drain well and pat dry with paper towel.
2.	Preheat the air fryer to 355 degrees F. Place the potatoes in a fryer basket.
3.	Cook for about 30 minutes.
4.	Meanwhile in a bowl, add tuna, yogurt, red chili powder, salt, black pepper and half of scallion and with a potato masher, mash the mixture completely.
5.	Remove the potatoes from the air fryer oven and place onto a smooth surface.
6.	Carefully, cut each potato from top side lengthwise.
7.	With your fingers, press the open side of potato halves slightly. Stuff the potato open portion with tuna mixture evenly.
8.	Sprinkle with the capers and remaining scallion. Serve immediately.

Fried Calamari

Prep: 8 Minutes • Cook Time: 7 Minutes • Total: 15 Minutes
Serves: 6-8
Ingredients
½ tsp. salt
½ tsp. Old Bay seasoning
1/3 C. plain cornmeal
½ C. semolina flour
½ C. almond flour
5-6 C. olive oil
1 ½ pounds baby squid
Directions:
1.	Rinse squid in cold water and slice tentacles, keeping just ¼-inch of the hood in one piece.
2.	Combine 1-2 pinches of pepper, salt, Old Bay seasoning, cornmeal, and both flours together. Dredge squid pieces into flour mixture and place into the air fryer basket.
3.	Spray liberally with olive oil. Cook 15 minutes at 345 degrees till coating turns a golden brown.
PER SERVING: CALORIES: 211; CARBS:55; FAT: 6G; PROTEIN:21G; SUGAR:1G

Soy and Ginger Shrimp

Prep: 8 Minutes • Cook Time: 10 Minutes • Total: 15 Minutes
Serves: 4
Ingredients
2 tablespoons olive oil
2 tablespoons scallions, finely chopped
2 cloves garlic, chopped
1 teaspoon fresh ginger, grated
1 tablespoon dry white wine
1 tablespoon balsamic vinegar
1/4 cup soy sauce
1 tablespoon sugar
1 pound shrimp
Salt and ground black pepper, to taste
Directions:
1.   To make the marinade, warm the oil in a saucepan; cook all ingredients, except the shrimp, salt, and black pepper. Now, let it cool.
2.   Marinate the shrimp, covered, at least an hour, in the refrigerator.
3.   After that, pour into the Oven rack/basket. Place the Rack on the middle-shelf of the Air fryer oven. Set temperature to 350°F, and set time to 10 minutes. Bake the shrimp at 350 degrees F for 8 to 10 minutes (depending on the size), turning once or twice. Season prepared shrimp with salt and black pepper and serve.

Panko-Crusted Tilapia

Prep: 5 Minutes • Cook Time: 10 Minutes • Total: 15 Minutes
Serves: 3
Ingredients
2 tsp. Italian seasoning
2 tsp. lemon pepper
1/3 C. panko breadcrumbs
1/3 C. egg whites
1/3 C. almond flour
3 tilapia fillets
Olive oil
Directions:
1.   Place panko, egg whites, and flour into separate bowls. Mix lemon pepper and Italian seasoning in with breadcrumbs.
2.   Pat tilapia fillets dry. Dredge in flour, then egg, then breadcrumb mixture.
3.   Add to the air fryer basket and spray lightly with olive oil.
4.   Cook 10-11 minutes at 400 degrees, making sure to flip halfway through cooking.
PER SERVING: CALORIES: 256; FAT: 9G; PROTEIN:39G; SUGAR:5G

Potato Crusted Salmon

Prep: 10 Minutes • Cook Time: 15 Minutes • Total: 25 Minutes
Serves: 4
Ingredients
1 pound salmon, swordfish or arctic char fillets, 3/4 inch thick
1 egg white
2 tablespoons water
1/3 cup dry instant mashed potatoes
2 teaspoons cornstarch
1 teaspoon paprika
1 teaspoon lemon pepper seasoning
Directions:
1.   Remove and skin from the fish and cut it into 4 serving pieces Mix together the egg white and water. Mix together all of the dry ingredients. Dip the filets into the egg white mixture then press into the potato mix to coat evenly.
2.   Pour into the Oven rack/basket. Place the Rack on the middle-shelf of the Air fryer oven. Set temperature to 360°F, and set time to 15 minutes, flip the filets halfway through.
PER SERVING: CALORIES:176; FAT: 7G; PROTEIN:23G; :5G

Salmon Croquettes

Prep: 5 Minutes • Cook Time: 10 Minutes • Total: 15 Minutes
Serves: 6-8
Ingredients
Panko breadcrumbs
Almond flour
2 egg whites
2 tbsp. chopped chives
2 tbsp. minced garlic cloves
½ C. chopped onion
2/3 C. grated carrots
1 pound chopped salmon fillet
Directions:
1.   Mix together all ingredients minus breadcrumbs, flour, and egg whites.
2.   Shape mixture into balls. Then coat them in flour, then egg, and then breadcrumbs. Drizzle with olive oil.
3.   Pour the coated salmon balls into the Oven rack/basket. Place the Rack on the middle-shelf of the Air fryer oven. Set temperature to 350°F, and set time to 6 minutes. Shake and cook an additional 4 minutes until golden in color.
PER SERVING: CALORIES: 503; CARBS:61g; FAT: 9G; PROTEIN:5G; SUGAR:4G

Snapper Scampi

Prep: 5 Minutes • Cook Time: 10 Minutes • Total: 15 Minutes
Serves: 4
Ingredients
4 (6-ounce) skinless snapper or arctic char fillets
1 tablespoon olive oil
3 tablespoons lemon juice, divided
½ teaspoon dried basil
Pinch salt
Freshly ground black pepper
2 tablespoons butter
cloves garlic, minced
Directions:
1.   Rub the fish fillets with olive oil and 1 tablespoon of the lemon juice. Sprinkle with the basil, salt, and pepper, and place in the air fryer oven basket.
2.   Set temperature to 360°F and grill the fish for 7 to 8 minutes or until the fish just flakes when tested with a fork. Remove the fish from the basket and put on a serving plate. Cover to keep warm. In a 6-by-6-by-2-inch pan, combine the butter, remaining 2 tablespoons lemon juice, and garlic. Cook in the air fryer oven for 1 to 2 minutes or until the garlic is sizzling. Pour this mixture over the fish and serve.
PER SERVING: CALORIES: 265; CARBS:1g; FAT: 11G; PROTEIN:39G; FIBER:0G

Thai Fish Cakes With Mango Relish

Prep: 5 Minutes • Cook Time: 10 Minutes • Total: 15 Minutes
Serves: 4
Ingredients
1 lb White Fish Fillets
3 Tbsps Ground Coconut
1 Ripened Mango
½ Tsps Chili Paste
Tbsps Fresh Parsley
1 Green Onion
1 Lime
1 Tsp Salt
1 Egg
Directions:
1.   To make the relish, peel and dice the mango into cubes. Combine with a half teaspoon of chili paste, a tablespoon of parsley, and the zest and juice of half a lime.
2.   In a food processor, pulse the fish until it forms a smooth texture. Place into a bowl and add the salt, egg, chopped green onion, parsley, two tablespoons of the coconut, and the remainder of the chili paste and lime zest and juice. Combine well
3.   Portion the mixture into 10 equal balls and flatten them into small patties. Pour the reserved tablespoon of coconut onto a dish and roll the patties over to coat.
4.   Preheat the Air Fryer oven to 390 degrees
5.   Place the fish cakes into the air fryer oven and cook for 8 minutes. They should be crisp and lightly browned when ready
6.   Serve hot with mango relish

Air Fryer Fish Tacos

Prep: 5 Minutes • Cook Time: 15 Minutes • Total: 20 Minutes
Serves: 4
Ingredients
1 pound cod
1 tbsp. cumin
½ tbsp. chili powder
1 ½ C. almond flour
1 ½ C. coconut flour
10 ounces Mexican beer
2 eggs
Directions:
Whisk beer and eggs together.
Whisk flours, pepper, salt, cumin, and chili powder together.
Slice cod into large pieces and coat in egg mixture then flour mixture.
Spray bottom of your air fryer oven basket with olive oil and add coated codpieces. Cook 15 minutes at 375 degrees.
Serve on lettuce leaves topped with homemade salsa.
PER SERVING: CALORIES: 178; CARBS:61g; FAT:10G; PROTEIN:19G; SUGAR:1G

Firecracker Shrimp

Prep: 10 Minutes • Cook Time: 8 Minutes • Total: 18 Minutes
Serves: 4
Ingredients
For the shrimp
1 pound raw shrimp, peeled and deveined
Salt
Pepper
1 egg
½ cup all-purpose flour
¾ cup panko bread crumbs
Cooking oil
For the firecracker sauce
⅓ cup sour cream
2 tablespoons Sriracha
¼ cup sweet chili sauce
Directions:
1.   Season the shrimp with salt and pepper to taste. In a small bowl, beat the egg. In another small bowl, place the flour. In a third small bowl, add the panko bread crumbs.
2.   Spray the air fryer oven basket with cooking oil. Dip the shrimp in the flour, then the egg, and then the bread crumbs. Place the shrimp in the air fryer basket. It is okay to stack them. Spray the shrimp with cooking oil.
3.   Set temperature to 390°F. Cook for 4 minutes. Open the air fryer oven and flip the shrimp. I recommend flipping individually instead of shaking to keep the breading intact. Cook for an additional 4 minutes or until crisp.
4.   While the shrimp is cooking, make the firecracker sauce: In a small bowl, combine the sour cream, Sriracha, and sweet chili sauce. Mix well. Serve with the shrimp.
PER SERVING: CALORIES: 266; CARBS:23g; FAT:6G; PROTEIN:27G; FIBER:1G

Sesame Seeds Coated Fish

Prep: 10 Minutes • Cook Time: 8 Minutes • Total: 18 Minutes
Serves:5
Ingredients
3 tablespoons plain flour
2 eggs
½ cup sesame seeds, toasted
½ cup breadcrumbs
1/8 teaspoon dried rosemary, crushed
Pinch of salt
Pinch of black pepper
3 tablespoons olive oil
5 frozen fish fillets (white fish of your choice)
Directions:
1.   In a shallow dish, place flour. In a second shallow dish, beat the eggs. In a third shallow dish, add remaining ingredients except fish fillets and mix till a crumbly mixture forms.
2.   Coat the fillets with flour and shake off the excess flour.
3.   Next, dip the fillets in egg.
4.   Then coat the fillets with sesame seeds mixture generously.
5.   Preheat the air fryer oven to 390 degrees F.
6.   Line an Air fryer basket with a piece of foil. Arrange the fillets into prepared basket.
7.   Cook for about 14 minutes, flipping once after 10 minutes.

Bacon Wrapped Scallops

Prep: 5 Minutes • Cook Time: 5 Minutes • Total: 10 Minutes
Serves: 4
Ingredients
1 tsp. paprika
1 tsp. lemon pepper
5 slices of center-cut bacon
20 raw sea scallops
Directions:
1.   Rinse and drain scallops, placing on paper towels to soak up excess moisture.
2.   Cut slices of bacon into 4 pieces.
3.   Wrap each scallop with a piece of bacon, using toothpicks to secure. Sprinkle wrapped scallops with paprika and lemon pepper.
4.   Spray air fryer basket with olive oil and add scallops.
5.   Cook 5-6 minutes at 400 degrees, making sure to flip halfway through.
PER SERVING: CALORIES: 389; CARBS:63g; FAT:17G; PROTEIN:21G; SUGAR:1G

Crispy Paprika Fish Fillets

Prep: 5 Minutes • Cook Time: 15 Minutes • Total: 20 Minutes
Serves: 4
Ingredients
1/2 cup seasoned breadcrumbs
1 tablespoon balsamic vinegar
1/2 teaspoon seasoned salt
1 teaspoon paprika
1/2 teaspoon ground black pepper
1 teaspoon celery seed
2 fish fillets, halved
1 egg, beaten
Directions:
1.   Add the breadcrumbs, vinegar, salt, paprika, ground black pepper, and celery seeds to your food processor. Process for about 30 seconds.
2.   Coat the fish fillets with the beaten egg; then, coat them with the breadcrumbs mixture.
3.   Pour the fish fillets into the Oven rack/basket. Place the Rack on the middle-shelf of the Air fryer oven. Set temperature to 350°F, and set time to 15 minutes.

Parmesan Shrimp

Prep: 5 Minutes • Cook Time: 10 Minutes • Total: 15 Minutes
Serves: 4
Ingredients
2 tbsp. olive oil
1 tsp. onion powder
1 tsp. basil
½ tsp. oregano
1 tsp. pepper
2/3 C. grated parmesan cheese
4 minced garlic cloves
pounds of jumbo cooked shrimp (peeled/deveined)
Directions:
1.   Mix all seasonings together and gently toss shrimp with mixture.
2.   Spray olive oil into the air fryer basket and add seasoned shrimp.
3.   Cook 8-10 minutes at 350 degrees.
4.   Squeeze lemon juice over shrimp right before devouring!
PER SERVING: CALORIES: 351; FAT:11G; PROTEIN:19G; SUGAR:1G

Flaky Fish Quesadilla

Prep: 10 Minutes • Cook Time: 12 Minutes • Total: 22 Minutes
Serves: 4
Ingredients
Two 6-inch corn or flour tortilla shells
1 medium-sized tilapia fillet, approximately 4 ounces
½ medium-sized lemon, sliced
½ an avocado, peeled, pitted and sliced
1 clove of garlic, peeled and finely minced
Pinch of salt and pepper
½ teaspoon of lemon juice
¼ cup of shredded cheddar cheese
¼ cup of shredded mozzarella cheese
Directions:
1.   Preheat the air fryer oven to 350 degrees.
2.   In the air fryer oven, grill the tilapia with a little salt and lemon slices in foil on high heat for 20 minutes.
3.   Remove fish in foil from the oven, and break the fish meat apart into bite-sized pieces with a fork – it should be flaky and chunky when cooked.
4.   While the fish is cooling, combine the avocado, garlic, salt, pepper, and lemon juice in a small mixing bowl; mash lightly, but don't whip - keep the avocado slightly chunky.
5.   Spread the guacamole on one of the tortillas, then cover with the fish flakes, and then with the cheese. Top with the second tortilla.
6.   Place directly on hot surface of the air frying basket.
7.   Set the air fryer oven timer for 6 minutes.
8.   After 6 minutes, when the air fryer shuts off, flip the tortillas onto the other side with a spatula; the cheese should be melted enough that it won't fall apart.
9.   Reset air fryer oven to 350 degrees for another 6 minutes.
10.   After 6 minutes, when the air fryer shuts off, the tortillas should be browned and crisp, and the fish, guacamole and cheese will be hot and delicious inside. Remove with spatula and let sit on a serving plate to cool for a few minutes before slicing.

Quick Fried Catfish

Prep: 5 Minutes • Cook Time: 15 Minutes • Total: 20 Minutes
Serves: 4
Ingredients
3/4 cups Original Bisquick™ mix
1/2 cup yellow cornmeal
1 tablespoon seafood seasoning
4 catfish fillets (4 to 6 ounces each)
1/2 cup ranch dressing
Lemon wedges
Directions:
1.   In a shallow bowl mix together the Bisquick mix, cornmeal, and seafood seasoning. Pat the filets dry, then brush them with ranch dressing.
2.   Press the filets into the Bisquick mix on both sides until the filet is evenly coated.
3.   Cook in your air fryer oven at 360 degrees for 15 minutes, flip the filets halfway through.
4.   Serve with a lemon garnish.
PER SERVING: CALORIES: 372; FAT:16G; PROTEIN:28G; FIBER:1.7G

Honey Glazed Salmon

Prep: 5 Minutes • Cook Time: 8 Minutes • Total: 13 Minutes
Serves: 2
Ingredients
1 tsp. water
3 tsp. rice wine vinegar
6 tbsp. low-sodium soy sauce
6 tbsp. raw honey
2 salmon fillets
Directions:
1.   Combine water, vinegar, honey, and soy sauce together. Pour half of this mixture into a bowl.
2.   Place salmon in one bowl of marinade and let chill 2 hours.
3.   Ensure your air fryer oven is preheated to 356 degrees and add salmon.
4.   Cook 8 minutes, flipping halfway through. Baste salmon with some of the remaining marinade mixture and cook another 5 minutes.
5.   To make a sauce to serve salmon with, pour remaining marinade mixture into a saucepan, heating till simmering. Let simmer 2 minutes. Serve drizzled over salmon!
PER SERVING: CALORIES: 348; FAT:12G; PROTEIN:20G; SUGAR:3G

Fish and Chips

Prep: 10 Minutes • Cook Time: 20 Minutes • Total: 30 Minutes
Serves: 4
Ingredients
4 (4-ounce) fish fillets
Pinch salt
Freshly ground black pepper
½ teaspoon dried thyme
1 egg white
¾ cup crushed potato chips
2 tablespoons olive oil, divided
1 russet potatoes, peeled and cut into strips
Directions:
1.   Pat the fish fillets dry and sprinkle with salt, pepper, and thyme. Set aside.
2.   In a shallow bowl, beat the egg white until foamy. In another bowl, combine the potato chips and 1 tablespoon of olive oil and mix until combined.
3.   Dip the fish fillets into the egg white, then into the crushed potato chip mixture to coat.
4.   Toss the fresh potato strips with the remaining 1 tablespoon olive oil.
5.   Use your separator to divide the air fryer basket in half, set temperature to 360°F, then fry the chips and fish. The chips will take about 20 minutes; the fish will take about 10 to 12 minutes to cook.
PER SERVING: CALORIES: 374; FAT:16G; PROTEIN:30G; FIBER:4G

Fish Sandwiches

Prep: 10 Minutes • Cook Time: 20 Minutes • Total: 30 Minutes
Serves: 4
Ingredients
lbs White Fish Fillets
1/4 Cup Yellow Cornmeal
1 Tsp Greek Seasoning
Salt and Pepper to taste
2 ½ Cups Plain Flour
2 Tsps Baking Powder
2 Cups Beer
4 Hamburger Buns
Mayonnaise
Lettuce Leaves
1 Tomato, sliced
1 Egg

Directions:
1.   Cut the fish fillets into burger patty sized strips. Season with salt and pepper to desired taste.
2.   In a medium bowl, mix together the beer, egg, baking powder, plain flour, cornmeal, Greek seasoning and additional salt and pepper
3.   Heat the air fryer oven to 340 degrees
4.   Place each seasoned fish strip into the batter, ensuring that it is well coated
5.   Place battered fish into the air fryer tray and cook in batches for 6 minutes or until crispy
6.   Compile the sandwich by topping each bun with mayonnaise, then a lettuce leaf, tomato slices, and finally the cooked fish strip.

Crab Cakes

Prep: 5 Minutes • Cook Time: 10 Minutes • Total: 15 Minutes
Serves: 4
Ingredients
8 ounces jumbo lump crabmeat
1 tablespoon Old Bay Seasoning
⅓ cup bread crumbs
¼ cup diced red bell pepper
¼ cup diced green bell pepper
1 egg
¼ cup mayonnaise
Juice of ½ lemon
1 teaspoon flour
Cooking oil

Directions:
1.   In a large bowl, combine the crabmeat, Old Bay Seasoning, bread crumbs, red bell pepper, green bell pepper, egg, mayo, and lemon juice. Mix gently to combine.
2.   Form the mixture into 4 patties. Sprinkle ¼ teaspoon of flour on top of each patty.
3.   Place the crab cakes in the air fryer oven. Spray them with cooking oil. Set temperature to 390°F and cook for 10 minutes.
4.   Serve.

Crispy Air Fried Sushi Roll

Prep: 10 Minutes • Cook Time: 5 Minutes • Total: 15 Minutes
Serves: 12
Ingredients
Kale Salad:
1 tbsp. sesame seeds
¾ tsp. soy sauce
¼ tsp. ginger
1/8 tsp. garlic powder
¾ tsp. toasted sesame oil
½ tsp. rice vinegar
1 ½ C. chopped kale
Sushi Rolls:
½ of a sliced avocado
3 sheets of sushi nori
1 batch cauliflower rice
Sriracha Mayo:
Sriracha sauce
¼ C. vegan mayo
Coating:
½ C. panko breadcrumbs
Directions:
1.   Combine all of kale salad ingredients together, tossing well. Set to the side.
2.   Lay out a sheet of nori and spread a handful of rice on. Then place 2-3 tbsp. of kale salad over rice, followed by avocado. Roll up sushi.
3.   To make mayo, whisk mayo ingredients together until smooth.
4.   Add breadcrumbs to a bowl.
5.   Coat sushi rolls in crumbs till coated and add to the air fryer oven.
6.   Cook rolls 10 minutes at 390 degrees, shaking gently at 5 minutes.
7.   Slice each roll into 6-8 pieces and enjoy!
PER SERVING: CALORIES: 267; FAT:13G; PROTEIN:6G; SUGAR:3G

Sweet Recipes

Perfect Cinnamon Toast

Prep: 10 Minutes • Cook Time: 5 Minutes • Total: 15 Minutes
Serves: 6
Ingredients
2 tsp. pepper
1 ½ tsp. vanilla extract
1 ½ tsp. cinnamon
½ C. sweetener of choice
1 C. coconut oil
12 slices whole wheat bread
Directions:
1.   Melt coconut oil and mix with sweetener until dissolved. Mix in remaining ingredients minus bread till incorporated.
2.   Spread mixture onto bread, covering all area.
3.   Pour the coated pieces of bread into the Oven rack/basket. Place the Rack on the middle-shelf of the Air fryer oven. Set temperature to 400°F, and set time to 5 minutes.
4.   Remove and cut diagonally. Enjoy!
PER SERVING: CALORIES: 124; FAT:2G; PROTEIN:0G; SUGAR:4G

Easy Baked Chocolate Mug Cake

Prep: 5 Minutes • Cook Time: 15 Minutes • Total: 20 Minutes
Serves: 3
Ingredients
½ cup cocoa powder
½ cup stevia powder
1 cup coconut cream
1 package cream cheese, room temperature
1 tablespoon vanilla extract
1 tablespoons butter
Directions:
1.   Preheat the air fryer oven for 5 minutes.
2.   In a mixing bowl, combine all ingredients.
3.   Use a hand mixer to mix everything until fluffy.
4.   Pour into greased mugs.
5.   Place the mugs in the fryer basket.
6.   Bake for 15 minutes at 350°F.
7.   Place in the fridge to chill before serving.
PER SERVING: CALORIES: 744; FAT:69.7G; PROTEIN:13.9G; SUGAR:4G

Angel Food Cake

Prep: 5 Minutes • Cook Time: 30 Minutes • Total: 35 Minutes
Serves: 12
Ingredients
¼ cup butter, melted
1 cup powdered erythritol
1 teaspoon strawberry extract
12 egg whites
2 teaspoons cream of tartar
A pinch of salt
Directions:
1.   Preheat the air fryer oven for 5 minutes.
2.   Mix the egg whites and cream of tartar.
3.   Use a hand mixer and whisk until white and fluffy.
4.   Add the rest of the ingredients except for the butter and whisk for another minute.
5.   Pour into a baking dish.
6.   Place in the air fryer basket and cook for 30 minutes at 400°F or if a toothpick inserted in the middle comes out clean.
7.   Drizzle with melted butter once cooled.
PER SERVING: CALORIES: 65; FAT:5G; PROTEIN:3.1G; FIBER:1G

Fried Peaches

Prep: 2 Hours 10 Minutes • Cook Time: 15 Minutes • Total: 15 Minutes
Serves: 4
Ingredients
4 ripe peaches (1/2 a peach = 1 serving)
1 1/2 cups flour
Salt
2 egg yolks
3/4 cups cold water
1 1/2 tablespoons olive oil
2 tablespoons brandy
4 egg whites
Cinnamon/sugar mix
Directions:
1.   Mix flour, egg yolks, and salt in a mixing bowl. Slowly mix in water, then add brandy. Set the mixture aside for 2 hours and go do something for 1 hour 45 minutes.
2.   Boil a large pot of water and cut and X at the bottom of each peach. While the water boils fill another large bowl with water and ice. Boil each peach for about a minute, then plunge it in the ice bath. Now the peels should basically fall off the peach. Beat the egg whites and mix into the batter mix. Dip each peach in the mix to coat.
3.   Pour the coated peach into the Oven rack/basket. Place the Rack on the middle-shelf of the Air fryer oven. Set temperature to 360°F, and set time to 10 minutes.
4.   Prepare a plate with cinnamon/sugar mix, roll peaches in mix and serve.
PER SERVING: CALORIES: 306; FAT:3G; PROTEIN:10G; FIBER:2.7G

Apple Dumplings

Prep: 10 Minutes • Cook Time: 25 Minutes • Total: 35 Minutes
Serves: 4
Ingredients
2 tbsp. melted coconut oil
2 puff pastry sheets
1 tbsp. brown sugar
2 tbsp. raisins
2 small apples of choice
Directions:
1.   Ensure your air fryer oven is preheated to 356 degrees.
2.   Core and peel apples and mix with raisins and sugar.
3.   Place a bit of apple mixture into puff pastry sheets and brush sides with melted coconut oil.
4.   Place into the air fryer. Cook 25 minutes, turning halfway through. Will be golden when done.
PER SERVING: CALORIES: 367; FAT:7G; PROTEIN:2G; SUGAR:5G

Apple Pie in Air Fryer

Prep: 5 Minutes • Cook Time: 35 Minutes • Total: 40 Minutes
Serves: 4
Ingredients
½ teaspoon vanilla extract
1 beaten egg
1 large apple, chopped
1 Pillsbury Refrigerator pie crust
1 tablespoon butter
1 tablespoon ground cinnamon
1 tablespoon raw sugar
2 tablespoon sugar
2 teaspoons lemon juice
Baking spray
Directions:
1.   Lightly grease baking pan of air fryer oven with cooking spray. Spread pie crust on bottom of pan up to the sides.
2.   In a bowl, mix vanilla, sugar, cinnamon, lemon juice, and apples. Pour on top of pie crust. Top apples with butter slices.
3.   Cover apples with the other pie crust. Pierce with knife the tops of pie.
4.   Spread beaten egg on top of crust and sprinkle sugar.
5.   Cover with foil.
6.   For 25 minutes, cook on 390°F.
7.   Remove foil cook for 10 minutes at 330oF until tops are browned.
8.   Serve and enjoy.
PER SERVING: CALORIES: 372; FAT:19G; PROTEIN:4.2G; SUGAR:5G

Air Fryer Chocolate Cake

Prep: 5 Minutes • Cook Time: 35 Minutes • Total: 40 Minutes
Serves: 8-10
Ingredients
½ C. hot water
1 tsp. vanilla
¼ C. olive oil
½ C. almond milk
1 egg
½ tsp. salt
¾ tsp. baking soda
¾ tsp. baking powder
½ C. unsweetened cocoa powder
2 C. almond flour
1 C. brown sugar
Directions:
1.   Preheat your air fryer oven to 356 degrees.
2.   Stir all dry ingredients together. Then stir in wet ingredients. Add hot water last.
3.   The batter will be thin, no worries.
4.   Pour cake batter into a pan that fits into the fryer. Cover with foil and poke holes into the foil.
5.   Bake 35 minutes.
6.   Discard foil and then bake another 10 minutes.
PER SERVING: CALORIES: 378; FAT:9G; PROTEIN:4G; SUGAR:5G

Banana-Choco Brownies

Prep: 5 Minutes • Cook Time: 30 Minutes • Total: 35 Minutes
Serves: 12
Ingredients
2 cups almond flour
2 teaspoons baking powder
½ teaspoon baking powder
½ teaspoon baking soda
½ teaspoon salt
1 over-ripe banana
3 large eggs
½ teaspoon stevia powder
¼ cup coconut oil
1 tablespoon vinegar
1/3 cup almond flour
1/3 cup cocoa powder
Directions:
1.   Preheat the air fryer oven for 5 minutes.
2.   Combine all ingredients in a food processor and pulse until well-combined.
3.   Pour into a baking dish that will fit in the air fryer.
4.   Place in the air fryer basket and cook for 30 minutes at 350°F or if a toothpick inserted in the middle comes out clean.
PER SERVING: CALORIES: 75; FAT:6.5G; PROTEIN:1.7G; SUGAR:2G

Chocolate Donuts

Prep: 5 Minutes • Cook Time: 20 Minutes • Total: 25 Minutes
Serves: 8-10
Ingredients
(8-ounce) can jumbo biscuits
Cooking oil
Chocolate sauce, such as Hershey's
Directions:
1.   Separate the biscuit dough into 8 biscuits and place them on a flat work surface. Use a small circle cookie cutter or a biscuit cutter to cut a hole in the center of each biscuit. You can also cut the holes using a knife.
2.   Spray the air fryer basket with cooking oil.
3.   Place 4 donuts in the air fryer oven. Do not stack. Spray with cooking oil. Set temperature to 350°F. Cook for 4 minutes.
4.   Open the air fryer and flip the donuts. Cook for an additional 4 minutes.
5.   Remove the cooked donuts from the air fryer oven, then repeat for the remaining 4 donuts.
6.   Drizzle chocolate sauce over the donuts and enjoy while warm.
PER SERVING: CALORIES: 181; FAT:98G; PROTEIN:3G; FIBER:1G

Easy Air Fryer Donuts

Prep: 5 Minutes • Cook Time: 5 Minutes • Total: 10 Minutes
Serves: 8
Ingredients
Pinch of allspice
4 tbsp. dark brown sugar
½ - 1 tsp. cinnamon
1/3 C. granulated sweetener
3 tbsp. melted coconut oil
1 can of biscuits
Directions:
1.   Mix allspice, sugar, sweetener, and cinnamon together.
2.   Take out biscuits from can and with a circle cookie cutter, cut holes from centers and place into air fryer.
3.   Cook 5 minutes at 350 degrees. As batches are cooked, use a brush to coat with melted coconut oil and dip each into sugar mixture.
4.   Serve warm!
PER SERVING: CALORIES: 209; FAT:4G; PROTEIN:0G; SUGAR:3G

Chocolate Soufflé for Two

Prep: 5 Minutes • Cook Time: 14 Minutes • Total: 19 Minutes
Serves: 2
Ingredients
2 tbsp. almond flour
½ tsp. vanilla
3 tbsp. sweetener
2 separated eggs
¼ C. melted coconut oil
3 ounces of semi-sweet chocolate, chopped
Directions:
1.   Brush coconut oil and sweetener onto ramekins.
2.   Melt coconut oil and chocolate together.
3.   Beat egg yolks well, adding vanilla and sweetener. Stir in flour and ensure there are no lumps.
4.   Preheat the air fryer oven to 330 degrees.
5.   Whisk egg whites till they reach peak state and fold them into chocolate mixture.
6.   Pour batter into ramekins and place into the air fryer oven.
7.   Cook 14 minutes.
8.   Serve with powdered sugar dusted on top.
PER SERVING: CALORIES: 238; FAT:6G; PROTEIN:1G; SUGAR:4G

Fried Bananas with Chocolate Sauce

Prep: 10 Minutes • Cook Time: 10 Minutes • Total: 20 Minutes
Serves: 2
Ingredients
1 large egg
¼ cup cornstarch
¼ cup plain bread crumbs
3 bananas, halved crosswise
Cooking oil
Chocolate sauce (see Ingredient tip)
Directions:
1.   In a small bowl, beat the egg. In another bowl, place the cornstarch. Place the bread crumbs in a third bowl. Dip the bananas in the cornstarch, then the egg, and then the bread crumbs.
2.   Spray the air fryer basket with cooking oil. Place the bananas in the basket and spray them with cooking oil.
3.   Set temperature to 360°F and cook for 5 minutes. Open the air fryer and flip the bananas. Cook for an additional 2 minutes. Transfer the bananas to plates.
4.   Drizzle the chocolate sauce over the bananas, and serve.
5.   You can make your own chocolate sauce using 2 tablespoons milk and ¼ cup chocolate chips. Heat a saucepan over medium-high heat. Add the milk and stir for 1 to 2 minutes. Add the chocolate chips. Stir for 2 minutes, or until the chocolate has melted.
PER SERVING: CALORIES: 203; FAT:6G; PROTEIN:3G; FIBER:3G

Apple Hand Pies

Prep: 5 Minutes • Cook Time: 8 Minutes • Total: 13 Minutes
Serves: 6
Ingredients
15-ounces no-sugar-added apple pie filling
1 store-bought crust
Directions:
1.   Lay out pie crust and slice into equal-sized squares.
2.   Place 2 tbsp. filling into each square and seal crust with a fork.
3.   Pour into the Oven rack/basket. Place the Rack on the middle-shelf of the Air fryer oven. Set temperature to 390°F, and set time to 8 minutes until golden in color.
PER SERVING: CALORIES: 278; FAT:10G; PROTEIN:5G; SUGAR:4G

Chocolaty Banana Muffins

Prep: 5 Minutes • Cook Time: 25 Minutes • Total: 35 Minutes
Serves: 12
Ingredients
¾ cup whole wheat flour
¾ cup plain flour
¼ cup cocoa powder
¼ teaspoon baking powder
1 teaspoon baking soda
¼ teaspoon salt
2 large bananas, peeled and mashed
1 cup sugar
1/3 cup canola oil
1 egg
½ teaspoon vanilla essence
1 cup mini chocolate chips
Directions:
1.   In a large bowl, mix together flour, cocoa powder, baking powder, baking soda and salt.
2.   In another bowl, add bananas, sugar, oil, egg and vanilla extract and beat till well combined.
3.   Slowly, add flour mixture in egg mixture and mix till just combined.
4.   Fold in chocolate chips.
5.   Preheat the air fryer oven to 345 degrees F. Grease 12 muffin molds.
6.   Transfer the mixture into prepared muffin molds evenly and cook for about 20-25 minutes or till a toothpick inserted in the center comes out clean.
7.   Remove the muffin molds from Air fryer and keep on wire rack to cool for about 10 minutes. Carefully turn on a wire rack to cool completely before serving.

Blueberry Lemon Muffins

Prep: 5 Minutes • Cook Time: 10 Minutes • Total: 15 Minutes
Serves: 12
Ingredients
1 tsp. vanilla
Juice and zest of 1 lemon
2 eggs
1 C. blueberries
½ C. cream
¼ C. avocado oil
½ C. monk fruit
2 ½ C. almond flour
Directions:
1 Mix monk fruit and flour together.
In another bowl, mix vanilla, egg, lemon juice, and cream together. Add mixtures together and blend well. Spoon batter into cupcake holders.
2 Place in air fryer oven. Bake 10 minutes at 320 degrees, checking at 6 minutes to ensure you don't overbake them.
PER SERVING: CALORIES: 317; FAT:11G; PROTEIN:3G; SUGAR:5G

Sweet Cream Cheese Wontons

Prep: 5 Minutes • Cook Time: 5 Minutes • Total: 10 Minutes
Serves: 16
Ingredients
1 egg mixed with a bit of water
Wonton wrappers
½ C. powdered erythritol
8 ounces softened cream cheese
Olive oil
Directions:
1. Mix sweetener and cream cheese together.
2. Lay out 4 wontons at a time and cover with a dish towel to prevent drying out.
3. Place ½ of a teaspoon of cream cheese mixture into each wrapper.
4. Dip finger into egg/water mixture and fold diagonally to form a triangle. Seal edges well.
5. Repeat with remaining ingredients.
6. Place filled wontons into the air fryer oven and cook 5 minutes at 400 degrees, shaking halfway through cooking.
PER SERVING: CALORIES: 303; FAT:3G; PROTEIN:0.5G; SUGAR:4G

Air Fryer Cinnamon Rolls

Prep: 15 Minutes • Cook Time: 5 Minutes • Total: 15 Minutes
Serves: 8
Ingredients
1 ½ tbsp. cinnamon
¾ C. brown sugar
¼ C. melted coconut oil
1 pound frozen bread dough, thawed
Glaze:
½ tsp. vanilla
1 ¼ C. powdered erythritol
2 tbsp. softened ghee
ounces softened cream cheese
Directions:
1. Lay out bread dough and roll out into a rectangle. Brush melted ghee over dough and leave a 1-inch border along edges.
2. Mix cinnamon and sweetener together and then sprinkle over dough.
3. Roll dough tightly and slice into 8 pieces. Let sit 1-2 hours to rise.
4. To make the glaze, simply mix ingredients together till smooth.
5. Once rolls rise, place into air fryer and cook 5 minutes at 350 degrees.
6. Serve rolls drizzled in cream cheese glaze. Enjoy!
PER SERVING: CALORIES: 390; FAT:8G; PROTEIN:1G; SUGAR:7G

Bread Pudding with Cranberry

Prep: 5 Minutes • Cook Time: 45 Minutes • Total: 50 Minutes
Serves: 4
Ingredients
1-1/2 cups milk
2-1/2 eggs
1/2 cup cranberries1 teaspoon butter
1/4 cup and 2 tablespoons white sugar
1/4 cup golden raisins
1/8 teaspoon ground cinnamon
3/4 cup heavy whipping cream
3/4 teaspoon lemon zest
3/4 teaspoon kosher salt
3/4 French baguettes, cut into 2-inch slices
3/8 vanilla bean, split and seeds scraped away
Directions:
1.   Lightly grease baking pan of air fryer with cooking spray. Spread baguette slices, cranberries, and raisins.
2.   In blender, blend well vanilla bean, cinnamon, salt, lemon zest, eggs, sugar, and cream. Pour over baguette slices. Let it soak for an hour.
3.   Cover pan with foil.
4.   For 35 minutes, cook on 330°F.
5.   Let it rest for 10 minutes.
6.   Serve and enjoy.
PER SERVING: CALORIES: 581; FAT:23.8G; PROTEIN:15.8G; SUGAR:7G

Black and White Brownies

Prep: 10 Minutes • Cook Time: 20 Minutes • Total: 30 Minutes
Serves: 8
Ingredients
1 egg
¼ cup brown sugar
2 tablespoons white sugar
2 tablespoons safflower oil
1 teaspoon vanilla
¼ cup cocoa powder
⅓ cup all-purpose flour
¼ cup white chocolate chips
Nonstick baking spray with flour
Directions:
1.   In a medium bowl, beat the egg with the brown sugar and white sugar. Beat in the oil and vanilla.
2.   Add the cocoa powder and flour, and stir just until combined. Fold in the white chocolate chips.
3.   Spray a 6-by-6-by-2-inch baking pan with nonstick spray. Spoon the brownie batter into the pan.
4.   Pour the pan into the Oven rack/basket. Place the Rack on the middle-shelf of the Air fryer oven. Set temperature to 390°F, and set time to 20 minutes. Bake for 20 minutes or until the brownies are set when lightly touched with a finger. Let cool for 30 minutes before slicing to serve.
PER SERVING: CALORIES: 81; FAT:4G; PROTEIN:1G; FIBER:1G

French Toast Bites

Prep: 5 Minutes • Cook Time: 15 Minutes • Total: 20 Minutes
Serves: 8
Ingredients
Almond milk
Cinnamon
Sweetener
3 eggs
4 pieces wheat bread
Directions:
1. Preheat the air fryer oven to 360 degrees.
2. Whisk eggs and thin out with almond milk.
3. Mix 1/3 cup of sweetener with lots of cinnamon.
4. Tear bread in half, ball up pieces and press together to form a ball.
5. Soak bread balls in egg and then roll into cinnamon sugar, making sure to thoroughly coat.
6. Place coated bread balls into the air fryer oven and bake 15 minutes.

PER SERVING: CALORIES: 289; FAT:11G; PROTEIN:0G; SUGAR:4G

Baked Apple

Prep: 5 Minutes • Cook Time: 20 Minutes • Total: 25 Minutes
Serves: 4
Ingredients
¼ C. water
¼ tsp. nutmeg
¼ tsp. cinnamon
1 ½ tsp. melted ghee
2 tbsp. raisins
2 tbsp. chopped walnuts
1 medium apple
Directions:
1. Preheat your air fryer to 350 degrees.
2. Slice apple in half and discard some of the flesh from the center.
3. Place into frying pan.
4. Mix remaining ingredients together except water. Spoon mixture to the middle of apple halves.
5. Pour water over filled apples.
6. Place pan with apple halves into the air fryer oven, bake 20 minutes.

PER SERVING: CALORIES: 199; FAT:9G; PROTEIN:1G; SUGAR:3G

Coffee And Blueberry Cake

Prep: 5 Minutes • Cook Time: 35 Minutes • Total: 40 Minutes
Serves: 6
Ingredients
1 cup white sugar
1 egg
1/2 cup butter, softened
1/2 cup fresh or frozen blueberries
1/2 cup sour cream
1/2 teaspoon baking powder
1/2 teaspoon ground cinnamon
1/2 teaspoon vanilla extract
1/4 cup brown sugar
1/4 cup chopped pecans
1/8 teaspoon salt
1-1/2 teaspoons confectioners' sugar for dusting
3/4 cup and 1 tablespoon all-purpose flour
Directions:
1. In a small bowl, whisk well pecans, cinnamon, and brown sugar.
2. In a blender, blend well all wet Ingredients. Add dry Ingredients except for confectioner's sugar and blueberries. Blend well until smooth and creamy.
3. Lightly grease baking pan of air fryer with cooking spray.
4. Pour half of batter in pan. Sprinkle half of pecan mixture on top. Pour the remaining batter. And then topped with remaining pecan mixture.
5. Cover pan with foil.
6. For 35 minutes, cook on 330°F.
7. Serve and enjoy with a dusting of confectioner's sugar.
PER SERVING: CALORIES: 471; FAT:24G; PROTEIN:4.1G; SUGAR:6G

Cinnamon Sugar Roasted Chickpeas

Prep: 5 Minutes • Cook Time: 10 Minutes • Total: 15 Minutes
Serves: 2
Ingredients
1 tbsp. sweetener
1 tbsp. cinnamon
1 C. chickpeas
Directions:
1. Preheat air fryer oven to 390 degrees.
2. Rinse and drain chickpeas.
3. Mix all ingredients together and add to air fryer.
4. Pour into the Oven rack/basket. Place the Rack on the middle-shelf of the Air fryer oven. Set temperature to 390°F, and set time to 10 minutes.
PER SERVING: CALORIES: 111; FAT:19G; PROTEIN:16G; SUGAR:5G

Cherry-Choco Bars

Prep: 5 Minutes • Cook Time: 15 Minutes • Total: 20 Minutes
Serves: 8
Ingredients
¼ teaspoon salt
½ cup almonds, sliced
½ cup chia seeds
½ cup dark chocolate, chopped
½ cup dried cherries, chopped
½ cup prunes, pureed
½ cup quinoa, cooked
¾ cup almond butter
1/3 cup honey
2 cups old-fashioned oats
2 tablespoon coconut oil
Directions:
1.   Preheat the air fryer oven to 375°F.
2.   In a mixing bowl, combine the oats, quinoa, chia seeds, almond, cherries, and chocolate.
3.   In a saucepan, heat the almond butter, honey, and coconut oil.
4.   Pour the butter mixture over the dry mixture. Add salt and prunes.
5.   Mix until well combined.
6.   Pour over a baking dish that can fit inside the air fryer.
7.   Cook for 15 minutes.
8.   Let it cool for an hour before slicing into bars.
PER SERVING: CALORIES: 321; FAT:17G; PROTEIN:7G; SUGAR:5G

Cinnamon Fried Bananas

Prep: 5 Minutes • Cook Time: 10 Minutes • Total: 15 Minutes
Serves: 2-3
Ingredients
1 C. panko breadcrumbs
3 tbsp. cinnamon
½ C. almond flour
3 egg whites
8 ripe bananas
3 tbsp. vegan coconut oil
Directions:
1.   Heat coconut oil and add breadcrumbs. Mix around 2-3 minutes until golden. Pour into bowl.
2.   Peel and cut bananas in half. Roll each bananas half into flour, eggs, and crumb mixture.
3.   Place into the air fryer oven. Cook 10 minutes at 280 degrees.
4.   A great addition to a healthy banana split!
PER SERVING: CALORIES: 219; FAT:10G; PROTEIN:3G; SUGAR:5G

Coconutty Lemon Bars

Prep: 5 Minutes • Cook Time: 25 Minutes • Total: 30 Minutes
Serves: 12
Ingredients
¼ cup cashew
¼ cup fresh lemon juice, freshly squeezed
¾ cup coconut milk
¾ cup erythritol
1 cup desiccated coconut
1 teaspoon baking powder
2 eggs, beaten
2 tablespoons coconut oil
 air fryer of salt
Directions:
1.   Preheat the air fryer oven for 5 minutes. In a mixing bowl, combine all ingredients. Use a hand mixer to mix everything. Pour into a baking dish that will fit in the air fryer.
2.   Bake for 25 minutes at 350°F or until a toothpick inserted in the middle comes out clean.
PER SERVING: CALORIES: 118; FAT:10G; PROTEIN:2.6G; SUGAR:5G

CPSIA information can be obtained
at www.ICGtesting.com
Printed in the USA
LVHW100831150321
681563LV00019B/677